REBUILDING
a Jewel

SUCCESSFUL STRATEGIES FOR REVITALIZING HISTORIC PLACES

LYDIA K. ATUBEH

Ke'n L'chaim Llc
www.kenlchaimhistoricbuildings.com

Copyright © 2013 by Lydia K. Atubeh

All rights reserved. Written permission must be secured from the publisher to use or reproduce any part of this book, except for brief quotations in critical reviews or articles. It is illegal to copy this material, post it to a website, or distribute it by any other means without permission from the publisher. Forwarding or re-distribution of this publication is prohibited.

The author/publisher shall not be liable for misuse of this material. This book is strictly for informational and educational purposes. The author/publisher shall have neither liability nor responsibility to anyone with respect to any loss or damage caused or alleged to be caused, directly or indirectly by the information contained in this publication.

Published by Ke'n L'chaim LLC.

Ke'n L'chaim books may be purchased in bulk for educational, business, fundraising, or sales promotional use. For information, please email media@kenlchaim.com

ISBN-10: 0615988598
ISBN-13: 978-0615988597

Verses identified as NIV are taken from **THE HOLY BIBLE, NEW INTERNATIONAL VERSION®, NIV® Copyright © 1973, 1978, 1984, 2011 by Biblica, Inc.®** Used by permission. All rights reserved worldwide.

Unless otherwise noted the images and illustrations included in this publication were completed by Lydia K. Atubeh. Images by others were used by permission.

Front Cover Image: Jerusalem, Israel

TABLE OF CONTENTS

Acknowledgements — v

1 Introduction — 1
- *The Changing Urban Built Environment* — 4
- *How to Use This Book* — 10

2 The Role of Revitalization — 15
- *Why Revitalize?* — 15
- *How Can Changes Be Made?* — 17

3 Planning for Historic Places — 25
- *A Management Practice* — 25
- *Conservation in the UK Planning System* — 29
- *The International Influence* — 33
- *Conservation & Regeneration in England* — 37
- *Public Involvement* — 43

4 Durham, England: Connecting Heritage with Revitalization Goals — 47
- *Durham: Planning and Conservation* — 47
- *The Durham Regeneration Master Plan* — 56

    The Sites: Market Place, Elvet Waterside & former Ice Rink (Kascada Bowl)   59

    Influence Mapping & Stakeholder Analysis   78

    The Assessment of Public Value   86

5 Emerging Themes   89

    Stakeholder Analysis and Influence Map   93

6 The Global Revitalization Landscape: A Further Look   99

    Bastrop, Louisiana (United States)   100

    Jaffa (Yafo), Israel   112

7 Conclusion   129

Bibliography   137

Appendices   155

    A. Completing A Stakeholder Analysis   155

    B. The Influence Map   157

Acknowledgements

This book is possible because of the help of many. I first thank God for giving me continued strength for the project and I thank my family and friends for their enthusiasm, dedication and support.

Thanks to my advisor at the University of York, Sophie Norton, for her encouragement during my postgraduate studies and continued support after graduation. Thanks also go to Martin Lowe, Nicola Duckworth, Andrew Inch and Peter Herbert, Durham County Council, for providing information on the sites in this study. Thank you to Michael Hurlow, Durham City Vision, for contributions on the regeneration program and the three sites investigated. Thanks to Douglas Pocock for input on the work of the City of Durham Trust and to Alan Hunter for his insight on the work of English Heritage and its involvement in the regeneration of Durham. Thanks to Colin Wilkes, Durham Markets, Durham Forum and Durham City Chamber of Trade, for his views on the impact of the regeneration on local businesses.

Thanks to Christopher Downs for sharing the conservation work of Durham Cathedral, Seif El-Rashidi, Durham World Heritage site, for his openness in providing resources that added clarity to my understanding of the city and its relationship to the World Heritage complex and to Peter Robinson, Durham University, for providing essential information on the university's historic buildings and the redevelopment of Elvet Waterside. Thanks to Linda Curtis and Calvin Hedley, County Durham Society for the Blind and Partially Sighted, for adding the perspective of the disabled population.

I extend my appreciation to Betty Alford-Olive (previous Bastrop Mayor), Marc Vereen (Bastrop Main Street), Kay King (Morehouse Economic Development Corporation) and Susan Arnett (business owner), for their willingness to provide information on the regeneration program in their city, Bastrop, Louisiana, United States. Special thanks to Anglo-Israel Archaeological Society for providing travel support to Israel for research. Thanks to Tamar Tuchler (Society for Preservation of Israel Heritage Sites) and Rotem Zevi (freelance conservation professional) for the information provided on the regeneration work in Jaffa (Yafo) and for their hospitality during my stay in Israel.

Thanks to Lauren Adkins and Pam Briggs, National Trust for Historic Preservation Main Street Center, for information on its activities and current work.

Make no little plans. They have no magic to stir men's blood...Make big plans; aim high in hope and work...

--Daniel Burnham, Architect & Urban Designer

1 Introduction

During the 2013 conference of the United States/International Council on Monuments and Sites (US/ICOMOS) (an organization focused on the preservation of international heritage), the chief executive of the American Planning Association (APA), Paul Farmer, presented the findings of a national poll conducted by the APA over the previous year. The organization found that most residents in a community wanted five main elements to be improved as part of planning programs: "job creation, safety, neighborhoods, education and water quality" (Farmer 2013). The APA also created an infographic, breaking down the main areas in which individuals wanted to see progress.

One of the staggering statistics brought forth from the survey was that "84 percent felt their community [was] getting worse or [was] staying the same" and overall had not improved over the last five years (APA 2012). A revitalization or regeneration program for neighborhoods was considered only moderately important, but essential aspects that are typically the focus of improvement in revitalization, such as improving the economic activity and increasing the amount of green or energy-efficient dwellings for families,

2   *Rebuilding A Jewel: Successful Strategies for Revitalizing Historic Places*

Figure 1 Period townhouses along Montgomery Street in a historic district in Savannah, Georgia. The city was the location of the US/ICOMOS 16th annual symposium.

were key areas for many. In response to a conferee's question regarding the cause of this lower ranking of revitalization, Farmer stated that some of the previous renewal programs that communities had experienced did not fully accomplish what the neighborhoods as a whole had initially envisioned. These types of occurrences had somewhat colored the attitudes and responses of survey respondents and affected the priority level at which revitalization was ranked. Instead, individuals focused on major facets of their community such as economic stability, citizen participation in planning, and a sense of well-being for all residents.

The findings of the APA essentially point further to a need for tool refinement, customized to focus on a community's residents and the areas they find important. The concerns noted illustrated some changes that are not only occurring within the United States (US) but also in other countries. Unemployment rates have continued to increase or remain steady in a number of regions, crime is rampant with casualties the main conversation starter among neighbors, and educational systems are frequently scrutinized for their effectiveness in meeting budgetary guidelines while producing students who are able to compete in a global market.

Respondents also noted that they wanted more participation in the planning process, as they felt community participation and representatives from the area experiencing the program would be essential to ensuring a process that achieved the initial goals set forth. The APA's research reemphasizes the results of a 2006 conference in the United Kingdom (UK) that focused on heritage within the planning sector. The conference, entitled *"Capturing the Public Value of Heritage,"* included in its main results the need for focusing on public value in planning programs. The participants — practitioners and scholars from the fields of planning and heritage — concluded that embracing the opinions of the public, as well as educating the public on aspects of planning to equip them to participate in the process, will help produce effective and positive change within a program. This requires strategic management and sustainable planning. An interdisciplinary and global approach can be used to achieve these aims.

This book provides an overview of interdisciplinary tools for successful stakeholder integration in revitalization programs for historic cities and communities. In view of recent developments in the field, this book will point to several methods often used in other disciplines and countries that work to alleviate challenges, specifically when working to balance the needs of historic preservation and economic development. Case studies from Europe, the Middle East, and the United States will be presented. A detailed presentation of the tools is included as they are also effective aids that can be used to sustain the changes achieved during these types of programs, thereby maintaining and realizing the ultimate goals.

THE CHANGING URBAN BUILT ENVIRONMENT

The changes, social and economic, occurring in an urban area over time affect its built environment. As a city evolves architecturally, new construction takes place and impacts existing historic assets. This is prevalent in cities throughout the world and can provide a benefit or leave a negative mark on the area. Planning scholar Peter J. Larkham discusses this in his influential work *Conservation and the City*. He notes the challenges this creates for professionals and refers to the lack of a "generally accepted theory of how to manage urban landscapes for conservation -- and practice." Documents such as the "Vienna Memorandum on World Heritage and Contemporary Architecture -- Managing the Historic Urban Landscape," created in 2005, were an effort to provide a theoretical construct on an international level (Araoz 2008). Yet difficulties still exist for those striving to manage the historic environment globally.

Internationally, planning for urban historic cities has been approached in various ways. In Durham, England, the first case study of this book, the historic environment is managed through the "land use planning system" and "conservation planning." The former entails "general objectives...which are set out in legislation or in some document of legal or accepted standing" (Cullingworth and Nadin 2006). Architectural conservation scholars Bernard M.

Figure 2 The various stages of use and repair of these historic commercial buildings in Shreveport, Louisiana, illustrate the change in building needs and the built environment that is occuring in various cities.

Figure 3 A derelict building in Shreveport, Louisiana set for restoration as part of the city's revitalization program.

Figure 4 Restored historic storefronts in Shreveport, Louisiana.

Feilden and Jukka Jokilehto describe the latter as "an activity designed to bridge the preferred future to the present," often completed through management plans for a site or area. Across England, these two techniques have been enfolded into an overarching, consistent reevaluation system seen across the country in which the outcomes of the planning processes are evaluated to check their effectiveness. When demonstrated to be resolving issues, they are sustained; when not providing appropriate benefits, they are reassessed and a new planning program instituted.

Urban revitalization or regeneration programs are frequently part of the United Kingdom's (UK) general planning initiatives and have been developed across a number of governmental frameworks

-- regional, county, and city. These programs have been influenced over time by a number of factors including the living status of a town's residents, the economic decline of an area, and contemporary perceptions of the "best possible use of urban land" (Roberts 2000). Peter Roberts, a specialist in Spatial Sustainable Development, defines these types of planning programs as a technique for "the resolution of urban problems...which seeks to bring about lasting improvement in the economic, physical, social and environmental conditions of an area that has been subject to change."

Studies have shown that the historic environment has a crucial role in realizing the objectives of revitalization. The past, in its architectural and intangible forms, is often embraced because of its great impact on both the life of an individual and the development of an area. It is often used as part of tourism, one of the main revenue streams for municipalities, and is an essential element of plans to renew an area. Focus on heritage is imperative, as it can be an intense draw. Some individuals will travel a long distance to explore and experience a historic site with which they have a connection, for example, the iconic religious pilgrimages that have been made for numerous years to the site of the Holy Sepulchre in Jerusalem, Israel. In recent times the process is referred to as heritage tourism, the process of involving historic places within public administration tourism plans as a strategy in building budgetary resources. The revolving nature of cities makes the impact of historic places on social and financial climates a strong one, particularly when changes surface.

European planning scholar Rebecca Madgin has discussed the nature of urban change in terms of the "reconceptualisation of the historic urban environment" which has taken place over the last five decades. As she notes, the entry of "conservation-led regeneration schemes" illustrates the importance of retaining the historic fabric of cities as development is planned and initiated. English

Heritage, the advisory body on heritage matters to England's national government, has worked to encourage cities to incorporate their historic architecture into their regeneration plans. The organization argues that by doing so towns may reap a variety of benefits, including aiding local economies. The effects of using historic places in economic development projects have been witnessed and noted in a number of locales. Attention is now being turned to the outcomes and to whether the main goals of the projects have been advanced within the regions affected by the transformation.

Publications on the subject frequently include information on creating quality conservation-focused regeneration or revitalization programs. They present concise descriptions of case studies and provide evidence of the techniques needed in projects of this type. Yet there is a lack of scholarship on how to assess problems during the process and address them appropriately to ensure a positive outcome. As in the opening section of this book, communities are beginning to resist the revitalization program as a planning instrument and to focus instead on changing fundamental core areas where they reside. Existing literature focuses on three valuable means of eliminating challenges: stakeholder analyses, influence mapping, and methodologies connected to the "concept of public value" (Clark 2006b; Hammerton 2010). Stakeholder analyses and influence maps are noted as important in the project management field, and methodologies focused on providing public value are championed by heritage professionals working in the public sector.

The techniques of both the stakeholder analysis and influence mapping methodologies investigate the 1) individuals or groups affected by a project, 2) characteristics of the relationship between them and the decision makers, and 3) "variables such as trust and commitment" (Bourne and Walker 2005). The "analysis is an approach for understanding a system by identifying the key actors…and assessing their respective interests in, or influence on, that system" (Mayers 2005). Through an inspection of answers to questions such as Whose problem? or What are the power differences between stakeholders? solutions can be developed that build relationships so that positive instead of negative outcomes are gained.

The idea of public value stems from the work of Mark Moore, author of *Creating Public Value: Strategic Management in Government*. Moore, a mainstay in the public administration and academic sector, has addressed central points on the efficacy of government for public officials and the residents they serve. The scholar determines that success for public officials includes taking a holistic view of the citizen-focused system and changing from a general approach to a focus on *how* they deliver, engage, and envision the administrative process. This would also apply to heritage and the preservation of historic places. Kate Clark, a heritage and conservation professional in Australia, argues that utilizing the theoretical framework of public value is important for heritage, as heritage is something individuals value. She notes further that what "makes something part of our heritage is the value we place on it." Supporters of the theory have also stated that to use the concept organizations must not only consult the public regarding heritage matters but also truly engage them. This "process of engagement" is "not just about collecting data but deliberation and education" (Clark 2006b).

Renewal of a city or area requires a large number of individuals and resources. Gaining further understanding of the necessary factors needed to deliver a successful program is important for all in the historic preservation or conservation and planning sectors. With the political and financial climates currently experienced all over the globe, the planning landscape is at a tumultuous crossroads. In the United States the management of urban blight is a significant concern for many. Although the US housing market is beginning to resuscitate from its collapse in 2008, as of the writing of this book a number of cities are still on the verge of extinction. Residents are finding themselves alone among a series of derelict properties in various neighborhoods and suffering from reduced community resources and support. In Europe emergency and risk management plans are topping lists of immediate needs as areas long dormant and untouched by extreme weather conditions are experiencing violent earthquakes and floods. Throughout the Middle East, conflict among various cultures and regimes has put not only people but also heritage in danger as ancient structures are being destroyed while caught in the trajectories of firearms. Due to these circumstances and events, various initiatives are now forming the core of planning programs throughout the world. Efficiency is needed to balance the actions chosen to alleviate these issues and concerns. The present environment requires the incorporation of new ways of working to ensure the best use of time and funds, particularly for the protection of historic places.

The overall aim of this publication is to provide several keys to problem solving to those connected to the historic preservation and planning sectors. The tools that will be highlighted emphasize the importance of the stakeholder. These tools will enhance relationships among stakeholders and promote understanding of the factors contributing to issues that are experienced. It is hoped that stronger relationships between organizations and individuals can be cultivated. This publication also provides a more detailed view of the development of planning in England, Israel, and the United States. Included in these aims is an exploration of how the public value theoretical framework is used in a revitalization program.

How to Use This Book

This book is a call to action to reevaluate past approaches to revitalization or regeneration programs and to think globally, holistically, and traditionally, returning to the early roots of rebuilding a community. The material at the core of this publication is derived from my research and evaluation of the city revitalization program in Durham, England. The goals were to understand the relationships among stakeholders, the factors contributing to the challenges experienced, and resolutions to some of the difficulties that emerged throughout the process. The findings were evaluated and are presented here to demonstrate how they may be used to cultivate stronger relationships between organizations and individuals typically involved in such a project. Details regarding planning for heritage in the UK are included to provide the reader a context in which to understand the details of the revitalization project.

This book describes earlier tools as well as contemporary interdisciplinary methods to assess and manage conflict and reignite support for renewing areas. Two additional case studies from Israel

Figure 5 Rows of vacant buildings like these seen in Gary, Indiana are plaguing the US landscape. *(© Carolyn Richardson Atubeh)*

Figure 6 Neighborhoods in Gary, Indiana (shown above) have also suffered from slow decay and a reduction in their populations. Some homes have been boarded up and landscapes left to grow with no restraint. *(© Carolyn Richardson Atubeh)*

and Louisiana (USA) are included to further illustrate the value of such tools. This publication will help in several ways:

- Identifying all true stakeholders within a project, including their roles, interests, values, positions, and activities in the program.
- Utilizing effective conflict resolution tools during a renewal program.
- Gathering the foundational details of efforts that have already been completed to assess and encourage public value and determine what additional activities may be incorporated.
- Defining what initiatives or activities can be implemented to form or cultivate stakeholder relationships within a planned revitalization program.

They will rebuild the ancient ruins and restore the places long devastated; they will renew the ruined cities that have been devastated for generations.

Isaiah 61:4 NIV

These old buildings do not belong to us only, they belong to our forefathers and they will belong to our descendants unless we play them false. They are not in any sense our own property to do with as we like with them. We are only trustees for those that come after us.

--William Morris, Founding member of the Society for the Protection of Ancient Buildings

2 The Role of Revitalization

WHY REVITALIZE?

Revitalization has been a part of the history of the world since ancient times. In 445 B.C. a Jewish leader named Nehemiah led the restoration of the walls of Jerusalem in Israel and later the renewal of the city (Resig 2012). The initial phase of resurrecting the wall, the main entity protecting the city, took several elements: a strong vision, the support of governmental leaders, a comprehensive assessment of the state of the geographical area to be restored, the community, and lastly the education of the community on the issues and the support received for the reconstruction. This final step sealed the beginning of the work for the revitalization project. It was recorded that once the residents of the city understood the issues and were empowered to succeed, they were encouraged to begin.

Evidence of the influence of this early revitalization program is still seen through community-focused renewal projects of today. Some of the elements of Nehemiah's plan are becoming more a part of these types of projects in that they are typically supported by the local government. Mission and vision statements are fundamental

16 *Rebuilding A Jewel: Successful Strategies for Revitalizing Historic Places*

Figure 7 Modern day Jerusalem, Israel

to the effort, and the current state of the area is documented and used as a comparison in illustrating the end result of the program. The stakeholder involvement level has changed a great deal as the public is typically encouraged to participate by giving input on phase steps that have already been authorized and for which several design and outcome options have been created for review. This illustrates the increased focus on gaining support from residents but does not speak to sustaining this planning tool under emerging pressures being realized today.

Attitudes of those residing in historic cities and towns are gradually becoming more negative towards the changes that have been made through regenerating efforts. Community members are questioning the efficacy of these types of projects: Are they truly alleviating their concerns regarding their physical and social environments? This has led to quite contentious situations in some areas of the world. As referenced in APA's survey, revitalization programs currently are not seen as favorably by constituents as other planning efforts because previous programs did not fulfill anticipated results presented initially. Instead, constituents give priority to such amenities as education, water quality, and jobs, which typically formulate the necessity for revitalization programs.

Globally, these programs are termed in various ways: revitalization, regeneration, and renewal. Throughout this publication these terms will be used interchangeably. Most recently in some US heritage organizations the term *regenerating* has begun to emerge. How can these current situations of conflict or low confidence be rectified? Is a name change necessary? Do these programs need redefining?

Communication, education, and action are at the center of the resolution rather than the terminology. Additional tools are needed to cultivate sustainable management of this type of planning tool to ensure that the original intentions of the approach survive. Conflict that emerges may be resolved within planning for historic areas. Additional focus is needed on creating community environments where individuals empowered with concrete knowledge of the value they bring to the process are actually active within it. Historic cities have a great amount of significance attached to them, not only through their tangible built environment but also through intangible aspects such as their community values.

How Can Changes Be Made?

In the current political and societal climates, it is imperative to reassess current typical revitalization activities. The environmental and social changes referenced in the previous chapter have proven that a return to early forms of revitalization is beneficial and interdisciplinary methods of project management can bring about positive change. Since antiquity, scholars have chronicled the building and rebuilding of nations and their cities, thus providing detailed records and descriptions of early approaches to planning. In recent years the country of Italy has experienced massive earthquakes which destroyed many of its heritage sites. For example, in 2012 the *New York Times* noted that the region of Emilia-Romagna in northern Italy experienced an earthquake of great magnitude, its first in over 400 years. The region's previous major earthquake in 1570 prompted 16th-century architect and antiquarian Pirro Ligorio to create a document on constructing earthquake-resistant buildings, yet his ideas were not actually used until much later (Povoledo 2012). A return to these valuable sources is sorely needed.

As introduced at the beginning of this chapter, one of the earliest known rebuilding projects occurred in Jerusalem, Israel. Through the biblical account of Nehemiah, we learn that effective changes can be made even in challenging circumstances, and we see the benefits of the framework he established long ago.

A number of major elements contributed to the success of Nehemiah's early revitalization project:

1. Those engaging in a revitalization project must have a strong concern and compassion for the area and its community.

Economic vitality cannot be the sole motive; genuine compassion for the residents and temporary residents (tourists, students, etc.) must also be a priority. The main goal is to reestablish the vital function of the historic place, thus enabling its inhabitants to be successful and lead vibrant lives. Nehemiah was said to have wept and mourned for a number of days after hearing of the desolate condition of Jerusalem. His grief propelled him to seek God fervently for favor with the then ruling king (King Artaxerxes) who granted Nehemiah permission and safe passage to restore the fortress surrounding Jerusalem.

Projects of this scale may be initiated by a variety of entities: government, non-profits, or grassroots community efforts. Yet dedication and compassion for not only the historic place but also for the individuals connected to it -- as well as a vision to see the locale thrive -- must be at the core. This type of commitment is required to push through challenges that will arise and to ensure that obstacles that occur may be dealt with and new approaches explored when initial activities are no longer applicable or able to provide the initial expected results.

2. Governmental support is needed.

Elected or appointed officials related to an area at the national, state, or municipal levels are needed within the process. To gain an understanding of how they will influence a project, these officials should review previous projects and determine their funding sources. In Nehemiah's case, 13 years before the wall rebuilding project began, King Artaxerxes of Persia played an influential role when he granted Ezra the Scribe permission to return to Jerusalem and resume ceremonies in the Temple, the major religious building of the Jews in Jerusalem. Later, the king aided Nehemiah in his return to Jerusalem to restore the city's walls.

Funding is not the only prerequisite to an activity of this magnitude. It is said that King Artaxerxes provided Nehemiah with two letters, one requesting safe passage and one requesting timber for the rebuilding. Products and materials can be contributed by businesses within the immediate area, and artisans from the surrounding region may be engaged to contribute to the process. The restoration of poignant historic structures would be completed in service to the area as those involved would benefit from the resurrection of a place once desolate. Upon completion of the work, businesses will be able to create a solid customer base and increase revenues to an extent not achievable prior to the effort.

Often locations that are in dire need of a rebuilding effort suffer from ridicule and contempt in the form of nicknames with negative connotations. This can make it increasingly difficult to cultivate change and garner support. Area officials, however, can show initiative and encourage others in the community to work towards repositioning the neighborhood, city, or town by officially recognizing local civic leaders or groups. Renaming an area to emphasize its positive attributes may also be helpful.

3. Complete A Comprehensive Assessment.

The area to be revitalized needs a comprehensive assessment, typically completed at the quietest time of day or a time with the least amount of activity. This allows one to fully assess the condition of the location. Areas that have experienced the most intense amount of wear will be easier to view. It is recorded that Nehemiah explored the entire city walls by night while most were in their homes.

After assessing the area and before any work is begun, a report illustrating the urgency and necessity of the revitalization should be created and presented to a cross section of individuals throughout the geographical region. Those to receive this report would include community, government, and religious leaders as well as affluent members of the community and representatives of the construction industry and specialty trades.

Furthermore, a report provides the opportunity to put forth the idea of repositioning the area in the minds of residents first, before working to change the external views held by non-residents. Eliciting the support of the local residents and merchants is key to renewing their sense of purpose and increasing morale. Cultivating involvement in the rebuilding effort instead of simply disseminating information is crucial.

4. Cultivate an Engaging Presentation.

A presentation should be made showing the challenges and negative aspects of the historic place in its current condition, emphasizing how its degraded state invites mockery or contempt from others and creates low morale for residents.

Give a call to action to achieve a major milestone of the revitalization, for example, rebuilding the surrounding wall of the city or cleaning up the main corridors into the town with a focus on the landscape surrounding the buildings.

Demonstrate the troubling conditions of the proposed area, not only the dilapidated structures but also the economic and social health of all involved. It is vital at this point to explain that all will have a part in the process and that action will be the key element. The timeline in the beginning is important; however, initiating the project will be the first challenge. Those who do not want to participate will be the first hurdle, not unlike the first project in Jerusalem where those with alliances elsewhere did not want to see the city resurrected. Nehemiah, however, did not begin intense debates with these dissenters; instead, they were simply acknowledged, and the work continued. Once the majority of citizens understood the situation and the ramifications of continuing in the current condition, it is recorded that "they strengthened their hands for the good work" (Nehemiah 2:18 NIV).

5. Small Efforts Create Great Change.

Residents and business community members have an opportunity to make a great impression on their local area. Activities can be developed for residents to make a difference even if they cannot complete a full restoration of their property. According to the biblical book of Nehemiah, nobles, religious and political leaders, and those artisans not part of the construction trades completed the portion of the Jerusalem wall directly in front of their properties.

Figure 8 A shopping area in Jerusalem, Israel that has seen the adaptive reuse of a number of its period stone structures into retail spaces.

Residents within contemporary revitalization efforts could begin by focusing on their landscapes surrounding their property. As they develop and implement a low-maintenance environment, out-of-control vegetation in neighborhoods will decrease.

6. Reduce the focus on the negative.

The circumstances of the Jerusalem regeneration clouded the possibility of success. Several prominent individuals and groups in the area vehemently opposed the project, declaring it could not be accomplished, citing the large amount of deterioration the wall had suffered. Besides this negative publicity, a lack of building materials posed a problem, as the wall was only rubble at some points. Famine accompanied by economic recession also plagued Nehemiah's building program. Despite declining incomes, citizens were pressed to mortgage their lands and obtain loans with difficult terms in order to pay taxes. As this was beginning to cause a heavy strain on those participating in the rebuilding, a debt forgiveness plan was put into effect with full cooperation from loan holders. Everyone agreed that the debt was not benefiting the community as a whole and was breaking down the bonds that enabled participants to work together in the revitalization.

7. Prepare for Challenges.

Critics are everywhere in our society. We see them in media, politics, and even the food industry. They were also prevalent in antiquity. Nehemiah and the rebuilding of Jerusalem received numerous attacks from locals and individuals in neighboring geographical locations. Fearing what the project would do to them and their reputations, naysayers attempted to halt the program. They did not want to see Jerusalem reestablished and its residents thriving. Notably, Nehemiah refused to engage in deep debate with his critics but instead responded matter-of-factly to their numerous attempts to sabotage plans for the revitalization of Jerusalem. Their main intent was to intimidate and ultimately stop progress. We learn from Nehemiah that giving a simple response to negative publicity as opposed to carrying on detailed discussions works to disarm antagonists and quell these types of situations.

With city walls in ruins and homes unsafe to live in, Jerusalem became a vast revitalization and rebuilding project. Over the following chapters the points presented here will be highlighted to show how they have been put into place in several cities. Current mechanisms from fields not typically connected to preservation or revitalization can contribute to overcoming some of the challenges mentioned here.

...Stand at the crossroads and look; ask for the ancient paths, ask where the good way is, and walk in it, and you will find rest for your souls.
Jeremiah 6:16 NIV

We shape our buildings; thereafter, our buildings shape us.
     --Winston Churchill, Former Prime Minister of the United Kingdom

3 Planning for Historic Places

A Management Practice

Historic preservation or conservation planning is extensively related to revitalization as it focuses on the historic resources intrinsic to the renewal of an area. Terms used for this practice vary from one region of the world to another. *Historic preservation planning* is used predominantly in the US, and *conservation and management planning* is used in continents such as Europe and Australia.

At the core of each term used in planning is the assessment and recording of historic properties to gain an understanding of them. This then provides a foundation to articulate the next steps for repairs and the appropriate course of action for continued maintenance in the form of a preservation or management plan. The main difference between the planning terms is in the follow-up actions that take place after the assessment and planned development stages. For example, in locations that utilize the conservation planning process, change in the society, environment, and physical landscape propels the evolution of national or regional land use planning policies for the historic environment. With locations employing historic preservation planning, the majority of activity is at the local level and driven by county and city government agencies and civic organizations. In this publication the terms used are aligned with the country presented in the case study.

The planning practice has been explored in depth by several scholars, including James Semple Kerr, Bernard Feilden and Jukka Jokilehto, and has been defined as the processes involved in effectively managing the historic environment. Important aspects of conservation planning involve recognizing the significance of historic places through the application of designations and proposing legislation for their protection.

Some planning mechanisms include officially recognizing individual properties through a listing process or defining specific geographical locations as historic districts or conservation areas. Conservation and management plans, created as guides for sustaining the significance of historic sites and places, play an essential part (Clark 2001). Devised in response to investigations of the historic fabric, the plans provide detailed strategies for maintenance or restoration procedures.

Conservation planning has been argued to be a valuable activity in that it gives appropriate consideration to historic assets as opposed to general planning which takes into account overall land development. Feilden and Jokilehto (1998) note that "[conservation planning] is a critical element of the management of cultural resources." The importance of planning for historic buildings has also been outlined in recent years by the UK Department for Communities and Local Government (DCLG). The department notes that "planning has a central role to play in conserving our heritage assets and utilising the historic environment in creating sustainable places" (2010).

Policy development for heritage is strongly influenced not only by societal changes but also by the early roots of preservation. Countries like England however are consistently reworking their strategies in carrying out policy to accommodate changes in the economy, environment and society. Policies such as England's National Planning Policy Framework (NPPF), established in 2012, and the Historic Environment Planning Practice Guide, created in 2010, have taken into account prevailing thoughts in scholarship on categories such as sustainability and appropriate development in historic areas. The dominant intent of these policies is to ensure that changes made to structures do not affect what originally made them significant and that if adverse changes are unavoidable they will be implemented due to a great public need that will outweigh the adverse effect.

The policies also relate to previous literature on sustainable development. In 1987 the United Nations World Commission on Environment and Development published *Our Common Future*, also known as *The Brundtland Report*, one of the foundational pieces of literature on the subject. This document asserted that sustainable development is "development that meets the needs of present generations without compromising the ability of future generations to meet their own needs" (WCED 1987). Later scholars noted that sustainability refers to "long-term economic, environmental, and community health (Bauen et al. 1996). The NPPF advises that a city or region's development should focus on three main areas: the economic, social, and environmental (or physical), with the environmental portion relating to historic places. By including those three areas the framework thereby aligns with the main facets of sustainability and defines its role in regeneration.

A brief overview of the previously used policy documents from England is presented here to further illustrate the ongoing reevaluation process utilized. *Planning Policy Guidance (PPG) 15: Planning and the Historic Environment* (Department of the Environment and Department of National Heritage 1994) and *PPG 16: Archaeology and Planning* (DoE 1990) were developed initially to aid local governments in assisting residents and owners of historic properties

(Hobson 2004). *Planning Policy Statement (PPS) 5: Planning for the Historic Environment* (DCLG 2010) provided a more concise document and replaced *PPG 15* and *PPG 16*. Most recently the NPPF was instituted as a comprehensive tool, replacing *PPS 5*.

Another noteworthy aspect of conservation or historic preservation planning is communication. Communication may be argued to reside at the core of conservation. The transfer or "exchange of information" is fundamental to protecting the significance and values of historic assets (Merriam-Webster Online Dictionary 2010). Within the planning process various forms of communication are employed. Clark (2001) argues that facilitation and mediation as well as presentation are all part of conservation. Management procedures for a historic place may include a conservation plan that functions as a tool to express what steps should be instituted to care for the site. In other instances charters are used to convey how cultural heritage will be protected in coming years through periods of change (Marquis-Kyle and Walker 2004; Mynors 2006).

Communication has not been examined a great deal in studies on preservation or conservation planning. Malcolm Tait and Heather Campbell (2000) examined the subject within the general land use planning context. They completed an analysis of communication in a planning authority on the south coast of England among politicians, policy makers, and the planning officers who carry out the policies. Tait and Campbell state that a "focus on language [in planning] is important, as language does not just convey messages but can be seen as the way in which we construct meaning in the world. The extent to which language creates 'truth' can therefore influence what is seen as knowledge." Salvador Muñoz Viñas (2005) investigated the topic of communication in the field of conservation and noted a lack among occupations within the field. He determined a need for practitioners such as conservation scientists and curators of historic objects to engage in valuable dialogue to move forward in successfully protecting the objects under their care. Conclusions in both studies suggested more research on the topic is needed as unclear communication can be a barrier to efficiency within the preservation sector.

As the studies above highlight, communication has a role in conservation planning. The facets of conservation planning, legislation and policies, function as means of conveying how the historic environment may be protected. How this is established in the United Kingdom will be presented in the context of the Durham, England case study.

CONSERVATION IN THE UK PLANNING SYSTEM

Research completed by Barry Cullingworth and Vincent Nadin (2006) highlights the intricacies of conservation and the place it holds within the broader field of the UK planning system. Cullingworth and Nadin posit that the British system of planning tends to "embrace discretion" as it is generally thought that this encourages the ability to customize solutions to specific planning scenarios. An example of this was the previously used *PPS 5: Planning for the Historic Environment* (DCLG 2010), developed for the regional and local government levels to assist in the planning for historic places. The language of the document stipulated that the policies should influence the planning activities of local authorities. The current practice guide is now used in conjunction with the National Planning Policy Framework, and local governments are encouraged to use both documents to guide and inform development decisions and plans.

A range of statutes, initiatives, and advocacy documents were developed to institute concise and proactive means of protecting the historic environment. Planning lawyer Charles Mynors (2006) also argues that the policies created throughout history have made society aware of its heritage. Another area of importance is how the policies are used to manage the work that is completed on historic structures. A brief history provides an understanding of how these measures have been incorporated.

Conservation existed in legislative terms before town and country planning but was later "assimilated" into the system (Delafons 1997). In 1923 the Housing Etc. Act (HEA 1923) introduced the idea of the conservation area in England. The Act brought the phrase "special architectural, historic or artistic interest" into the planning language. Consideration of the character of historic assets in the development of towns began to emerge during this time. Officially, the term 'conservation area' was not declared until the 1967 Civic Amenities Act (CAA 1967) (Mynors 2006). Two decades after the introduction of the listing system for historic structures through the Town and Country Planning Act 1947 (TCPA 1947), conservation was seen as "an integral but relatively minor part of the planning system" (Delafons 1997; Mynors 2006).

It was not until 1968 that official listing and its protections were implemented (Hobson 2004; Mynors 2006). The Planning (Listed Buildings and Conservation Areas) Act 1990 (P(LBCA)A 1990) appears to have consolidated the place of the historic environment more firmly than in previous legislation. The Act implemented layers of protection for listed structures by requiring listed building or conservation area consent along with the systematic planning permission required for work to take place.

Both John Delafons (1997) and Edward Hobson (2004) acknowledge the importance of conservation and planning to the process of protecting historic assets. It has been argued that it is necessary to understand the time in which conservation statutes and policies were developed in order to assess why they were created. Delafons maintains that they were not simply created by government of its own accord but were influenced by the opinions of society, the economy, and other elements. Hobson investigates how the values at the core of the policies were maintained in actual practice. Described as a "reflection of deeper cultural attitudes to the past," the values are considered part of the main elements of conservation (Hobson 2004). He notes that there have been problems throughout the development of statutory frameworks for listed buildings and conservation areas which mainly center on the practices that have resulted from the statutory rulings. Hobson calls for a broader approach to conservation which would lead to its being seen as a cultural and environmental management program. He also notes that although essential information was learned through his research, more work is still required in the field.

Feilden and Jokilehto elaborate a great deal on the subject of conservation as part of town planning and outline the necessary objectives in planning for historic resources. One objective is initiating the process by integrating the idea of protecting the historic fabric of the buildings and considering them as part of the ongoing change and subsequent progress of a city. They argue that the core of an urban area must not be viewed as "static" or purely as a "tourist attraction" (Feilden and Jokilehto 1998). This point has also been made by Delafons (1997), who suggests that "conservation is part of planning [and] planning must incorporate conservation objectives" (Delafons 1997).

The ideals of conservation have been outlined by various means. The value systems and conservation philosophies stipulated by John Ruskin, Eugène-Emmanuel Viollet-le-duc, Alois Reigl, and Cesare Brandi have all contributed to this subject, helping to define the early history of conservation and providing a foundation for conservation philosophies in modern times. For some of the early scholars, the historic building or structure was considered a monument of the time in which it was created. Of particular significance is their discussion of the elements that contribute to the worth of a historic monument -- its inherent value and that imparted by society. This worth is what should guide plans for its care.

Unifying conservation principles and planning through an appropriate approach is essential. Feilden and Jokilehto argue that "the starting point for conservation planning must be the identification, based on careful study and analysis, of the historic fabric of [a] town." This idea connects to the value-based philosophies outlined previously. In a values-based approach a town would be viewed in a holistic manner. This concept of "integrated conservation" meshes the terms conservation and planning (Feilden and Jokilehto 1998). Feilden and Jokilehto suggest that the primary aim is the development of a conservation master plan for cities which would guide decisions and development so that the values of the city are retained and development does not have a negative effect.

This type of plan would be valuable in communicating to stakeholders the important factors required to conserve a town's historic places. For some cities and projects, however, this step of producing a conservation master plan is not completed. Literature describing the incorporation of this idea or activities to navigate a program through the challenges it encounters are not profuse.

The policies for historic places within the English planning system have evolved over the past decades due to a variety of societal factors. In the early part of the 20th century various groups and individuals recognized the need to define systems to ensure the longevity of the country's historic resources. Many authors, including Delafons (1997), Jokilehto (1999), Muñoz Viñas (2005), and Mynors (2006), have written about the contributions made by such organizations as the Society for the Protection of Ancient Buildings (SPAB) and such individuals as Sir John Lubbock to the early establishment of parliamentary acts and other protocols for areas and sites of historic importance.

The development of some of these policies has been influenced by charters and conventions produced on an international scale. The previous *PPS 5 Planning for the Historic Environment* (DCLG 2010) was constructed in compliance with agreed-upon duties of England as a signatory of the Granada, Valetta, Florence, and the United Nations Education, Scientific and Cultural Organization (UNESCO) World Heritage Conventions. The Conventions offer criteria by which participating countries can measure the application of their historic environment policies. They illustrate to national governments and subsequently to their residents the important aspects of various types of heritage in Europe and abroad (Jokilehto 1998; Mynors 2006). In the case of the World Heritage Convention, further mechanisms are required, including management plans in which UNESCO encourages that a "consensus [is sought] with all stakeholders including the local community" (Orbaşli 2008).

THE INTERNATIONAL INFLUENCE

The international heritage Conventions create a dialogue between those who compose the documents and those who decide how to use them in policy delivery. They also reflect the prominent debates in conservation throughout the recent past. Gustavo F. Araoz (2008) suggests that the "1960s could be said to be the decade of building theoretical consensus" and the "1990s the adoption of new heritage categories, such as cultural landscapes..." Developing guidelines to communicate the proper course to follow in regard to historic resources decreases the potential for ambiguity. This is vital when working with heritage, as situations can emerge within the social context surrounding a project that create challenges for all. These can appear at varying levels and can include "political tension" (Delafons 1997).

In addition to the international Conventions, charters have been produced in response to challenges in dealing with the historic environment. In 1931 the Athens Charter established on an international scale the basic principles to be reflected upon in the "preservation and restoration of ancient buildings" (Feilden and Jokilehto 1998). The Venice Charter, developed in 1964, updated and expanded the ideas of the Athens Charter (Feilden and Jokilehto 1998; Orbaşli 2008), reflecting the changes experienced in conservation throughout several decades.

In 1979 the Burra Charter was adopted by Australia ICOMOS (International Council on Monuments and Sites), with final revisions taking place in 1999 (Marquis-Kyle and Walker 2004).

Figure 9 As part of historic preservation or conservation planning, management plans are created for historic sites. Liverpool, England, a maritime city with four areas of its historic centre listed as a World Heritage (WH) site, received such a plan to assist in its care and maintenance.

Figure 10 View of Liverpool, England's Cathedral near the city's docks.

Inspired by the Venice Charter, the Burra Charter was developed to address conservation practices in Australia. The charter appears to have refocused management processes in the heritage sector internationally. A prevailing theme is the charter's emphasis on *why* something was created and its intrinsic values (West and Ansell 2010). The values are then connected and compiled to determine the overall significance of a place or structure. This concept of significance -- and the attendant onus on preserving the elements which give it that significance -- was paramount (Marquis-Kyle and Walker 2004). The charter suggests three main steps: 1) "understand significance," 2) "develop policy," and 3) "manage" (Marquis-Kyle and Walker 2004). Another major theme of the Charter is sustaining relationships through communication with all who are involved in conservation planning. This was noted as an essential element for ensuring protection and care.

Discussions surrounding World Heritage have also made an impact on planning. The production of World Heritage management plans, strongly recommended as part of the World Heritage List designation process, and the issues that came to light during their creation have led to additional documents such as the Vienna Memorandum in 2005 (Chris Blandford Associates 2006; Araoz 2008). The creators of the document have sought to establish an environment in which to put forth ideas that will help to combat the problems that are encountered.

Discussions on urban design are prevalent in much of planning literature. A great deal of scholarship highlights the emergence of a focus on the evolution of urban areas. Terms such as "urban renaissance" were frequent in these discussions (Urban Task Force 1999; 2005). While conservation is found to be important in this area of scholarship, particularly as part of managing change in cities and the subsequent treatment of the historic fabric, it is still not described as a prominent part of the process. In 2012 the United Nations Educational, Scientific and Cultural Organization (UNESCO) worked to rectify this by officially signing into effect the *Recommendation on the Historic Urban Landscape*. The organization states the *Recommendation* is a "tool to integrate policies and practices of conservation of the built environment into the wider goals of urban development" (UNESCO World Heritage Centre 2012). Dr. Ron van Oers, the Vice Director of the World Heritage Institute of Training and Research in the Asia-Pacific region, further describes the *Recommendation* : He states, "in the approach, the urban area is understood as extending beyond the notion of 'historic centre' or 'district' to include the broader urban context and topographical setting, as well as social and cultural practices and values, economic processes and the intangible dimensions of heritage" (The News 2014).

In 2013 UNESCO published *New Life for Historic Cities* to provide further information on the *Recommendation*. The publication noted the fundamental steps included in the approach: 1) "undertake a full assessment of [a] city's natural, cultural and human resources," 2) utilize "participatory planning and stakeholder consultations" to obtain the values inherent in the resources, 3) "assess the vulnerability of urban heritage to socio-economic pressures...and climate change," 4) integrate the information gathered into "a wider framework of city development," 5) "prioritize policies and actions for conservation and development," 6) "establish the appropriate (public-private) partnerships and local management frameworks," and coordinate action between the sectors.

In close review the various parts of the *Recommendation* are very similar to the Burra Charter. The Charter also highlights the importance of creating an inventory of the historic assets of a community and assessing the values inherent in the assets.

Together, the Burra Charter and the *Recommendation*'s steps re-emphasize the need for policy to assist in taking action. Integrating policy is typically a more manageable process with historic places that have been designated for quite some time and are accepted in a society's culture. Yet, in locales where there are challenging circumstances such as the economy, raising awareness of the tangible and intangible values that exist within historic fabric to encourage protection through policy becomes difficult without inclusion of all connected stakeholders. In a later section several tools will be highlighted that can work towards resolving these types of issues.

Conservation & Regeneration in England

In the aftermath of World War II, throughout the 1950s and 1960s, England underwent a great deal of redevelopment (Jagger 1998; Madgin 2010).

The renowned town planner Thomas Sharp (1940) was very vocal prior to and during these regeneration periods. He argued that planning should continue to take place during difficult periods, such as times of unrest and war, as clear goals would help to focus planning efforts. Sharp praised the talents of 18th-century town planners in England who structured cities to help residents retain the balance between work and leisure, but he noted that the planners of the post-WWII period did not have these goals. In an effort to guide the process, he developed plans for several major areas, focusing on London and Liverpool.

Plans like those of Sharp and others during the time tended to focus on utilizing the historic environment but were frequently shelved because of opposition to these projects, meaning that many areas did not witness sensitive development (Sharp 1940; Pendlebury 2009). Resistance to chosen plans was initiated in large part by civic societies and preservation trusts along with others from the non-profit sector (Jagger 1998). Many felt that elements of their cities, especially those that were part of the historic environment, were being eliminated along with the character of the town or area (Hobson 2004).

The idea of fusing historic assets into the plans to regenerate the social and economic climates of English towns began to be realized again in the 1990s. An Urban Task Force was developed to promote an urban renaissance in cities throughout England (Urban Task Force 1999; 2005). The goals of the group were to establish and make recommendations on what needed to be done to regenerate the dilapidated areas of various cities. The major steps were to be undertaken by the government, but it was acknowledged that all levels and sectors would be involved in achieving the ideals set forth (Urban Task Force 2005).

English Heritage (1998) also produced research on urban renewal. The organization published information on conservation-led regeneration and its role in incorporating the concept into the development and conservation dialogue. In 2000 a collection of organizations involved in the heritage sector published *Power of Place: The Future of the Historic Environment* (Power of Place Office 2000). The central mission of the document was to outline the process of conservation-led development. The authors contended that the historic environment was important to many people, as confirmed by a MORI study commissioned to learn the public's opinion of the value of historic resources (Power of Place Office 2000). Statements by organizations in the field provided concrete evidence and statistics to construct a compelling case for the integration of historic places in urban and regional development.

Power of Place included recommendations on what would need to be accomplished to solidify the future of not only architectural heritage but also historic landscapes and other cultural resources. It demonstrated that a conservation-led philosophy was necessary and could contribute much to the economic regeneration goals of local authorities and regional development entities. Following the dissemination of the document, the House of Commons (2004) created *The Role of Historic Buildings in Urban Regeneration*. The publication continued where *Power of Place* ended. Its purpose was to determine what needed to be completed to successfully incorporate the idea of conservation into regeneration plans. The committees involved took an international perspective to learn what had been done in projects in other countries. Organizations in England were also polled for their views on what they felt was essential to incorporating conservation ideas outlined in previous scholarship in the field.

The goals of the project covered several themes, including the role of local government in regeneration, how historic resources were incorporated in regeneration programs, and the need for possible modifications to legislation. Some of the conclusions pointed to the need for local authorities to begin planning how they would use their historic buildings in regenerating their towns. The authors also acknowledged that local governments would need guidance on how to develop the right applications to move forward. Additional ideas included establishing redevelopment teams comprised of "conservation, planning and transport officers alongside regeneration specialists and experts in development finance" (House of Commons 2004).

Literature from the past 12 years illustrates that conservation has developed into a mainstay of regeneration programs. Organizations such as English Heritage have continued to champion the benefits of using historic places in regeneration projects through the publication of additional work on the subject, for example, its 2005 document *Regeneration and the Historic Environment: Heritage as a Catalyst for Better Social and Economic Regeneration*. The document includes an emphasis on the sustainable solutions conservation activities can provide.

In 1998 the Heritage Lottery Fund created the Townscape Heritage Initiative to aid in the regeneration of cities and towns in the United Kingdom through their historic architecture (Shipley *et al.* 2004). Part of the program's mission is to assist a "conservation area affected by economic and social deprivation" (Heritage Lottery Fund 2010). To gather funding for projects, the initiative utilizes a multi-stakeholder framework that includes such elements as management plans for a conservation area (Heritage Lottery Fund 2010). Additional aspects of projects funded may include efforts to understand the benefits of restoring a historic structure compared to its actual "market value," identified as its "conservation deficit" (Heritage Lottery Fund 2010).

As noted by Hobson (2004), the economic and political challenges that can arise during these programs have not been pursued

Planning for Historic Places   41

Figure 11 A view of Royal Albert Hall in London, England. The city was one of several for which prominent planner, Thomas Sharp, created plans.

in much of the existing literature. This gap in scholarship also relates to the communication challenges that can evolve between

Figure 12 A view of another important landmark in London, England, St. Paul's Cathedral.

decision makers and local communities regarding the regeneration plans being put into effect within cities. These problems can compound and ultimately stagnate a program. Discovering how to effectively combat these issues has become a prominent challenge in the heritage environment.

Public Involvement

The influence of the public is frequently cited in scholarship. In the development of design guides for a town or region, the opinions of the surrounding community are typically encouraged (Jagger 1998). These opinions are vital to understanding what is considered significant and are an aid to retaining what is considered valuable for residents. Members of the non-profit sector have argued that the role of such groups as civic organizations or Non Governmental Organizations (NGOs), which typically also include local community members, is important in moving the planning cause forward. It has been noted that in some instances financial assistance for projects can be procured through these channels when they are not available through commercial avenues (Heritage Link 2004). For example, in many parts of the world civic groups have sponsored the writing of books to educate the public on the history of a place or used their financial resources to obtain legal assistance to combat planned development that is likely to change a community's way of life or damage the characteristics that exemplify its historic value.

English Heritage (2006a; 2006b) also notes the importance of involving the local community to help establish a shared knowledge of the historic character of an area. In the development of conservation area character appraisals in England, public participation is a key component as it allows the demonstration of the importance of the historic environment and keeps those concerned involved. For example, in public meetings residents can voice their comments regarding the character appraisal. Such approaches have been prominent within the last decade, culminating in 2006 with a conference in London on the production of "public value" (Clark 2006a; 2006b, 2).

As noted in the introductory chapter of this book, the idea of creating public value was created by Mark Moore (1995 cited Clark 2006b) who argued that the main objective for public sector leaders is to create public value. Upon investigating what society deems important, public sector leaders must present benefits that the community will feel comfortable investing in and supporting. The conference entitled *"Capturing the Public Value of Heritage"* emphasized that the thoughts and opinions of the public towards the historic environment should be respected.

One of the theoretical frameworks presented at the conference contributed to an understanding of how this concept of public value could be developed and measured. Using the "refined preference" was seen to be key in providing public value (Blaug, Horner and Lekhi 2006). It was noted that "refined preference" takes place when the public authorizes and informs the heritage sector of its preferences. The heritage professionals can then educate the public to make informed decisions. The public value may be measured by the "capacity of an organisation to...respond to public preferences" (Blaug, Horner and Lekhi 2006). The idea covered a variety of instances in which this could take place: "educational initiatives," "consultations," and "surveys" (Blaug, Horner and Lekhi 2006).

Analyzing and reassessing how to develop value for the public is a vital part of managing the historic environment. Once it is known what a local civic organization or trust appreciates or needs, local governments can be empowered. This allows success in overall preservation planning agendas but particularly in revitalization programs. The approaches that stem from these lessons can help to create a more cohesive context in which conservation can work.

The topics covered previously – historic preservation or conservation planning, conservation as part of the regeneration dialogue, and the creation of public value – provide a foundation for the case studies to be presented: Durham, England; Bastrop, Louisiana (USA); and Jaffa, Israel. These case studies serve as a background to an understanding of how planning is executed for the historic environment, particularly within the city. The connecting thread through all the sections was how communication is manifested in the planning procedures for historic places. Stakeholders were also identified as valuable parts of the process, with relationships among them contributing to the outcome. It is hoped that this publication provides a further look into the field and additional knowledge to help accomplish the goals of planning for the historic environment.

Your people will rebuild the ancient ruins and will raise up the age-old foundations; you will be called Repairer of Broken Walls, Restorer of Streets with Dwellings.

Isaiah 58:12 NIV

If you show people the problems and you show people the solutions they will be moved to act.

--Bill Gates, Co-founder of Microsoft

4 Durham, England: Connecting Heritage with Revitalization Goals

The revitalization program in Durham, England offers an opportunity to view tools implemented internationally and to examine other strategies that can be applied in these types of programs. Although other countries will later be presented as well, the Durham city revitalization program includes a wide scope of approaches and stakeholders for such a project.

The aim of this chapter is to provide the reader a brief history of planning in Durham. The role of conservation within the system will be of particular focus. Later sections will present the regeneration master plan of the city and three of the sites which were part of the initial phase of the revitalization program. The outcomes obtained through the stakeholder analysis and influence mapping processes will conclude the chapter.

Durham: Planning and Conservation

The significance of Durham is due in large part to its historic architecture. Contributing to its over 550 statutorily designated buildings is the Durham Cathedral and Castle complex, added as a

Figure 13 A skyline view of Durham, England

World Heritage site in 1986 (Chris Blandford Associates 2006; BBC Wear 2 March 2010). The site is well established in the history of the city and has been the subject of numerous historical accounts of visits to Durham. The "cathedral and castle...were developed throughout the medieval period" (Chris Blandford Associates 2006). Many noted antiquarians throughout its past have described the city as pleasant and easy to navigate in spite of its hilly topography (Boyle 1892; Pocock 2006).

Thomas Sharp (1945), a prominent planning specialist, noted that before World War II Durham evolved rather "quietly." This was thought to be quite impressive as major changes in society such as the Industrial Revolution and the location of the city in a coal-dominated area were major influences. Peter Hilland (1978) stated that the wealth gained through coal during the 1800s resulted in the construction of townhouses on the periphery of the city. Later in the Victorian period the town saw larger streets and the establishment of a new institution, Durham University. Municipal archives contain evidence of Durham's progression before World War II, significantly during the early part of the 20th-century; for example, an addition to a blacksmith shop in 1904, the construction of an office in 1909, and improvements made to a forge and dwelling in 1920 (Durham County Record Office (DRO) ND/Du 13/6, 13/109 and 13/208). Yet in the 1930s, societal changes impacted architecture in Durham. These changes included the construction of "chain store architecture" and suburban areas outside the city (Sharp 1945).

Figure 14 Old Elvet in Durham, England

Durham, similar to other English cities, was subject to extensive town planning and development during and after WWII. During the 1940s Thomas Sharp (1945) was commissioned to create a plan for the city, focusing on retaining its historic architecture and depicting how new development should take place. He determined the needs of the city and submitted a design of what the new town would look like under his plan. He also compiled a list of planning recommendations, arguing against some of the developments that were underway at the time. Primarily, Sharp argued for the preservation of Durham's historic character, emphasizing the importance of its cathedral and castle. He advocated sensitive design of new buildings within the boundaries of the cathedral and castle site and affirmed the importance of other historic aspects of the city. For example, Sharp maintained that the 18th-century Georgian character, seen particularly on Old Elvet, pictured in Figure 14, should be preserved since the Georgian period exhibited thoughtful town planning. He cited the need for the adaptive reuse of buildings where previous uses were no longer viable and the development of a public trust to protect the future of the Georgian structures.

Sharp's influence can be seen in some of the later planning initiatives by the local government. At his suggestion general design guides were developed for various portions of the town. Hilland (1978) notes that these guides impacted design efforts of building owners in the city after the 1950s. They were also completed for those in the Durham city conservation area, designated in 1968 (English Heritage (EH) CHA/5197/0004). Currently, design briefs are created for individual sites proposed for development.

Throughout the 1960s and 1970s Durham witnessed a variety of changes in its government, conservation activities, and development efforts. During this time great strides were made in conserving the historic buildings in the Durham Cathedral and Castle complex. An extension was added to Durham University's Palace

Green Library which is now within the World Heritage site (Hilland 1978; Durham University News 4 September 2008). Acclaimed architect George Pace designed the extension and included "traditional materials (such as stone)...to make the building fit in with the Cathedral and Castle" (Durham World Heritage Site 2014). The city also worked to keep historic importance at the front of progress. Correspondence within the county planning department from 1969 highlights aspects of a feasibility plan for the redevelopment of two main streets. Connecting strongly with Sharp's vision, the plan cited the importance of preserving the "medieval and Georgian" character of the city, noting the sensitivity of construction within a conservation area (DRO CC/Planning 1297).

Yet, some projects in the conservation area were not deemed to be as sensitive. In one instance in 1969, the City of Durham Trust composed a letter to the County Clerk expressing concern for the suitability of windows on a building located in a conservation area (DRO CC/Planning 1298). During the 1970s the local city council appeared to retain the focus on conservation within their activities. Projects such as a shopping complex, the Milburngate Shopping Centre, were delayed to ensure that historic buildings within the boundaries of development were appropriately incorporated and cared for during the process (Hilland 1978). The end result of the shopping center project incorporated the adaptive reuse and restoration of several historic structures.

Rosemary Cramp and Tony Scott (1987) expound upon the changes that took place during this time and the effects that were seen in Durham. They note that after the reorganization of the local government in 1974 plans were devised with the larger urban context in mind. Although the city center was in great need of repair, the newly annexed areas outside the city's core also needed attention. The local government divided its focus and sought to make sure that vital needs were attended to in the city center -- needs such as retaining "the architectural heritage [that] would [have been] lost" if postponed to a future time (Cramp and Scott 1987). Such intent was exhibited through the response of the local authority to the deteriorated state of two "Georgian shops" on one of the streets leading to the World Heritage site (Hilland 1978). A "revolving fund" was created to acquire and restore the buildings, allocating the monies from their sale or lease to complete work on other buildings in need (Hilland 1978).

In recent periods conservation planning in Durham has been influenced by several layers of policies. Before the installation of the Planning and Compulsory Purchase Act 2004 (PCPA 2004), England's governmental planning structure varied somewhat within each county. Consequently, the policies impacting the government functions as they pertained to the historic environment in the city of Durham also varied. In addition to the national policies discussed in the previous chapter, Durham's conservation plans were also subject to the *Regional Planning Guidance for the Northeast (RPG1)* (Government Office for the Northeast 2002), the Durham County Structure Plan and the City of Durham Local Plan. The Structure Plan for the county was adopted in 1999 and the Local Plan in 1988, with later revisions disseminated in 2000 (Durham City Council, nd). These policies underscored the importance of the World Heritage site in Durham as well as the need to protect the historic places in its conservation area.

The PCPA 2004 created new measures for local authorities, the most substantial of which was the local development framework. This framework includes a "mandatory core strategy, site specific allocations and proposals map [and] discretionary action plans" (Cullingworth and Nadin 2006). County and district governments were joined into a unitary government in April 2009 (Office for National Statistics 2005). As part of its duties from the unification, Durham County Council is currently in the process of

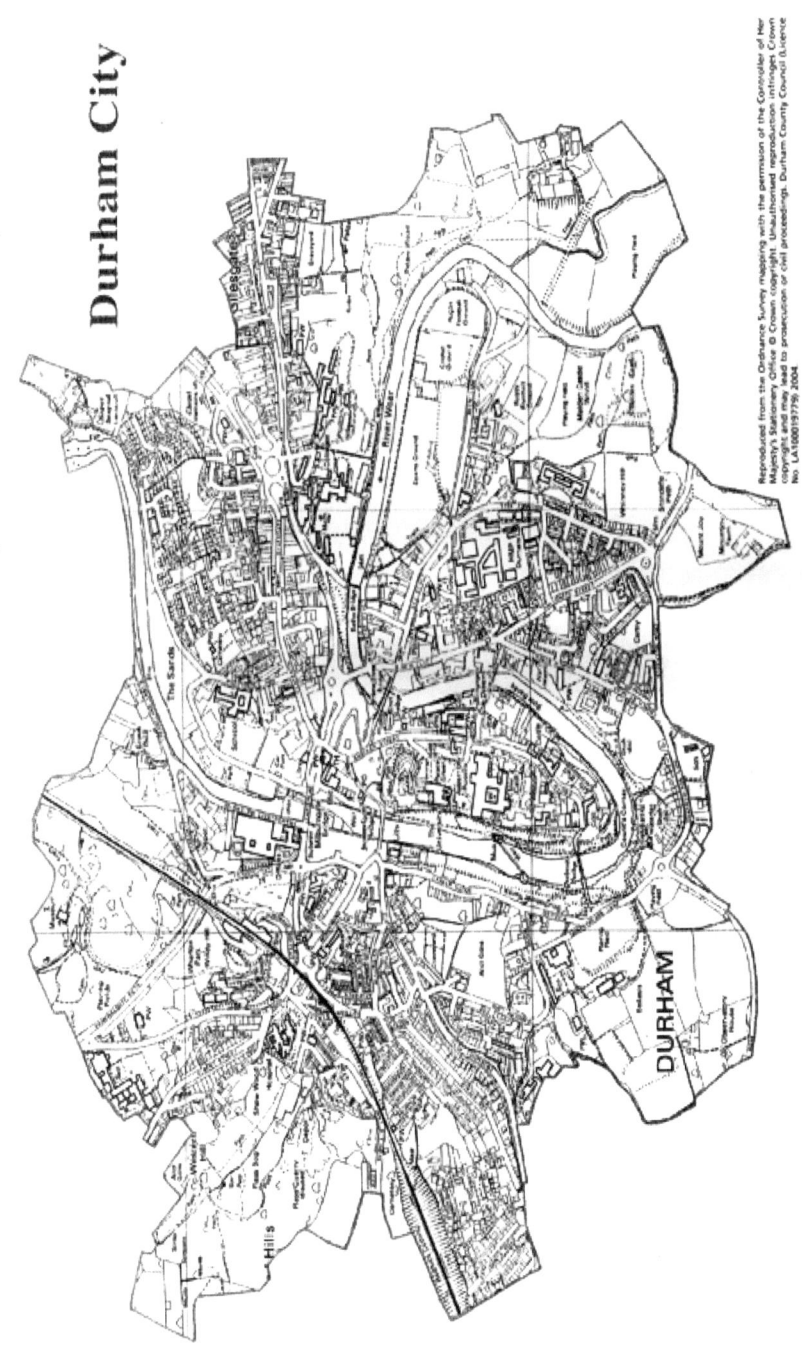

Figure 15 Durham City Conservation Area. (© *Durham County Council*)

developing the County Durham Plan (which will include the city of Durham) as required by the Planning and Compulsory Purchase Act. This planning instrument provides another layer of management in addition to the National Planning Policy Framework instituted in 2012 (Durham County Council 2013).

Some policies from the city's most recent local plan will continue to function as part of Durham's governing structure until the completion of the County Plan, currently scheduled for 2014 (Durham County Council 2013). Because of changes imposed by the redesign of the governmental structure, the local authority has worked to fully integrate the required departments and documents which guide their processes (Hurlow 2010). In the creation of the new core strategy, input from the residents of Durham city and the surrounding county is consistently being sought to make it viable for residents (Durham County Council 2010a; 2013).

Conservation is considered part of the planning process within Durham's local authority as planning applications with conservation area and listed building components are referred to specialists in the Design and Conservation section (Duckworth 2010; Inch 2010). The organizational structure for the municipality places the section in the Environmental and Planning department. The Design and Conservation area is one of 15 sections, along with archaeology and sustainability (Durham County Council 2013).

The conservation area within Durham city, Figure 15, encompasses the core of the city. English Heritage (CHA/5197/0004) records state that in 1980 the original boundaries were enlarged to "include the whole of the river bowl that provides the physical setting for the unique Durham City peninsula." This landscape feature, depicted in Figure 16, forms a unique part of the town. The protected area, entitled the Durham City Conservation Area, has not yet seen a conservation area character appraisal as part of its management process although the city is currently developing one

Figure 16 Landscape map of Durham, England (Imagery ©2014 Bluesky, DigitalGlobe, Getmapping plc, Infoterra Ltd & Bluesky, Map Data ©2014 Google)

(El-Rashidi 2013). This character appraisal, together with ideas from the local community, would provide guidance on how protections for the historic places would be incorporated for activities such as development (English Heritage 2006a).

A World Heritage site management plan was created for the cathedral and castle complex in 2006 (Chris Blandford Associates 2006). It provides direction for protecting the "outstanding universal value" of the complex and sustaining its use as a "religious, educational and residential" center (Chris Blandford Associates 2006). A coordinator is employed to organize the functions of the buildings, for example, visitor accessibility (El-Rashidi 2010).

The cathedral and Durham university, which owns the castle and a number of other buildings on the site, produced documents that contribute to managing their respective structures (Downs 2010; Robinson 2010). The cathedral and its adjacent buildings undergo an inspection every five years. After the investigation of the fabric of the buildings, a report is completed from which priorities are set for their conservation, and a working document is formed. The university has a similar program of regular inspections and a conditions survey every five years that prioritizes the works program. Each of the institutions has its own employees to provide restoration work on the buildings.

THE DURHAM REGENERATION MASTER PLAN

A Durham City master plan was developed in 2007 by Durham City Vision (DCV), the organization created in 2004 by the local government to complete the regeneration program. Since the plan's development was prior to the inception of the unitary government (Hurlow 2010), it was approved by the Durham City Council. The master plan was created to illustrate the focus of Durham's

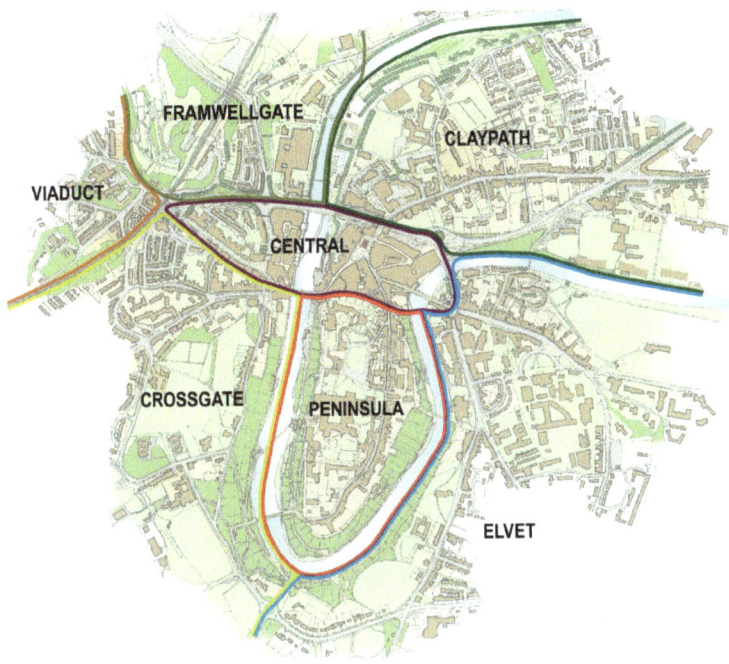

Figure 17 For the Durham regeneration program, a master plan was created. The plan's approach included breaking down the city into quarters and addressing the renewal of each one seperately.
(©*Durham City Vision*)

regeneration and to show how the project could be facilitated through a strategic approach. The document was also a comprehensive vision for Durham for the year 2020 (Durham City Vision 2007).

Through a breakdown of the city into quarters, Figure 17, the master plan presented concise information on what ideas have been formulated to improve various areas of the city. For each of the quarters, action steps were given to achieve the goals. Two years before the plan's publication, consultations were held to support its development. These took place through the help of a consultant, as well as "Durham Voices," a group representing the Durham city population (Durham City Vision 2007).

    This initial plan was the driver for the three sites that will be presented later in this chapter. Although Durham City Vision was dissolved in 2012, the following details form the basis of the first phases of work completed. The historic environment and its conservation was an essential part of the master plan. DCV explains within the document that historic architecture is an inherent part of Durham and therefore needs to be considered when contemplating its redevelopment. It argues the need to retain the historic significance of spaces and include the element of authenticity in the new plans but with modern design forming part of the final project. The organization states that the city is renowned for its World Heritage site and other historic architecture and that the plan is a tool to guide the development in light of the town's heritage. In descriptions of several of the town's quarters, histories of the areas are described using comments by well-known authors from the town's past, such as Thomas Sharp. This reinforces the historic character of the area and suggests that the planned development will be sensitive to historic places. Conservation management plans, such as the World Heritage management plan, are also noted. It is anticipated that the master plan and the plan for the World Heritage site will work together congruently.

    The main connection between the two plans is the implementation of new ways to draw visitors, the goal being to encourage tourists to engage with historic buildings and their settings. The early master plan included the development of a visitors center as well as a lighting program to improve the atmosphere and provide another layer to enhance the visitor's experience.

    Overall, the master plan defined what is possible for Durham's future and included goals for changes to the fabric of the city center -- its "places, spaces, buildings and activities" -- and to its "economic and social culture" (Durham City Vision 2007). DCV stated that the document was intended to aid the local government in creating a local development framework, noting that the city center is a common element among tourists and Durham residents. The master plan supported the initial steps of the regeneration of the area and contributed to making a positive experience for those in the local community -- residents, students, and visitors alike.

The protection and enhancement of historic assets is a continuing thread in the current master plan under development. The main emphasis, however, is on showcasing "the city's history, heritage, academic excellence and transport links" to encourage economic investment. Economic investment by companies and individuals, it is hoped, would enable the city to achieve success by increasing quality housing, improving education, and building on the city's "world-class" cultural roots. A community involvement strategy is now in place as of the date of this publication, with public comments being accepted for it as well as for the Durham County Plan.

THE SITES: MARKET PLACE, ELVET WATERSIDE & FORMER ICE RINK (KASCADA BOWL)

The three sites described in this section are representative of several projects currently underway as part of Durham's regeneration plan. Although the sites are in varying stages, they provide a picture of the work that is taking place and a context for understanding the most prominent stakeholders and the processes that have been conducted.

1. The Market Place

The first site to be presented, the Market Place, is one of the most comprehensive in the regeneration program. The location is shown in Figures 18 and 19. This site has been a central meeting point for the residents of Durham through most of its existence

Figure 18 View of street leading to the eastern portion of the Market Place (Durham, England).

Figure 19 The Market Place in Durham, England

Figure 20 The Market Place in Durham, England

(Durham City Vision 2007). Nikolaus Pevsner (1983), a prominent 20th-century art and architecture historian, attributes the character and charm of the Market Place to its unique location, describing it as the "crown of a hill." Pevsner describes several notable buildings that add significance to the Market Place, for example, "Gibson's National Provincial (National Westminster) Bank of 1876" and the prominent architectural features of two Georgian houses.

Peter Hilland (1978) also notes the depth of history that may be viewed through the Market Place. He notes the medieval period

Figure 21 The statue of Neptune within the Durham Market Place.

may be seen in "references from the street-lines, building heights and roof patterns" (Hilland 1978). Other elements of the historic environs of the Market Place include the statues of Lord Londonderry and Neptune, Figures 21 and 22, both of which are listed on the National Heritage List for England and have been a part of complex discussions on the development of the site

Figure 22 The statue of Lord Londonderry within the Durham Market Place. (© *Durham County Council/Durham City Vision*)

(Durham County Council (DCC) 09/00535/FPA). Urban planner Thomas Sharp (1945) discussed the significance of the Market Place holistically, stating that the "whole has a sturdy character that is well worth maintaining."

As part of the Durham regeneration, the Market Place has undergone a comprehensive treatment that has reorganized its layout, carried out the conservation of some of its current materials

Figure 23 The riven sandstone from the previous regeneration of the Durham Marketplace in 1973.

such as stone work, and initiated a grant program to encourage conservation of the surrounding properties (DCC 09/00535/FPA; Durham Times 14 May 2010; 30 March 2012). The Market Place transformation was officially initiated with the submission of the planning application in July 2009, and permission was granted in November 2009. Several months before the submission of the application, a comprehensive public consultation report was compiled to capture the opinions expressed by the local community during consultation meetings on the Market Place design.

During the time the planning application was open for public review, the project was commented on by a variety of local stakeholders (DCC 09/00535/FPA). Correspondence stemmed from organizations such as the City of Durham Trust and from current as well as previous residents of Durham. These categories of stakeholders -- the non-profit sector, local residents including

Figure 24 The new stone installed on the western side of the Marketplace.

temporary ones such as students and visitors, and the public sector -- will be highlighted in this section. Once stakeholder comments had been heard, the application underwent revisions prior to confirmation of the final project (Hurlow 2010).

Objections to the designs centered on several facets of the new plan: the proposed public seating for Market Place visitors, the floorscape, and the materials contemplated for use. The change in the positions of the listed statues and the way in which details of the regeneration plan were conveyed to the local community were further concerns. In 1973 the Market Place was the focus of a regeneration program which called for the installation of "local riven sandstone" as part of its floorscape (DCC 09/00535/FPA). This older stone was used in the main area of the Market Place as well as throughout its perimeter, Figure 23. Plans were put into place to clean and repair the sandstone surrounding most of the area, and replacements were installed on the western side of the space, depicted in Figure 24. The sandstone that was removed but not reused is set to be part of resurfacing plans in other parts of the city (DCC 09/00535/FPA).

Many of the initial objections to the floorscape noted that granite, the stone specified for the central portion of the space, would not fit within the historic character (DCC 09/00535/FPA). Flagstone was an alternative choice suggested as more suitable to the historic setting. A large portion of the Market Place floorscape is cobblestone, and although it is one of the original features, the stones have shifted over time and made the area problematic for pedestrians, particularly the disabled. Stakeholders raised safety concerns regarding the proposed pavement curb in the "pedestrian" area along the perimeter of the space, planned to be "laid level with other surfacing" (Tallentire 9 April 2010). Yet others, including representatives of the County Durham Society for the Blind and Partially Sighted, recalling the difficulties with the original design of the main space, endorsed the changes (Hedley 2010).

The listed statues were proposed to be moved a number of meters from their present locations to encourage more economic activity, such as event gatherings in the Market Place (Durham City Vision 2007). Although the dismantling and relocating of the statues would be considered demolition according to the P(LBCA)A 1990, after consulting *PPG 15: Planning and the Historic Environment* (DoE/DNH 1994), current at the time, the decision makers (Durham County Council and its partner organization Durham City

Vision) found that neither the statues nor their settings would be harmed. The statues have been part of the Market Place's history for over 100 years (DCC 09/00535/FPA). The figure of Neptune was moved to a nearby park for some time but was returned. The Lord Londonderry statue was a major subject of the local media due to its restoration shortly before the beginning of the project (Lloyd 16 October 2009). Many individuals expressed disappointment at the moving of the statues and felt it changed the ambiance of the space and that the statues would now compete with other listed buildings and original views within the Market Place (DCC 09/00535/FPA; Durham Times 22 January 2010).

Another essential aspect of the project was communication of the plans to the public prior to and during the early construction phases. Plans for the Market Place were announced through the media, such as local newspapers and the DCV website (Hurlow 2010). The consultation process for the designs began in November 2008 (Your Shout Communications 2009), but some Durham residents objected to the way in which information was delivered. They noted that valuable parts of the Market Place plan and the regeneration program were unknown to many in the community at the time the planning and listed building consent applications were made (DCC 09/00535/FPA). Others stated that prior to the consultations the details of the plan were not clear.

Durham Residents requested that the decision makers engage more with the public. Before and during the early work on the Market Place, business owners noted the challenges posed to normal operations, such as the construction zones in front of store fronts (Wilkes 2010). Durham Markets Company suggested that discussions with local merchants be increased to ensure that the economic viability of the Market Place is retained throughout the regeneration of the historic area.

As a major stakeholder, English Heritage also took part in the project, fulfilling its remit to monitor all projects involving demolition of Grade II listed structures and development of over 1,000 square meters (English Heritage 2009). The Market Place project met these criteria since the dismantling of the Lord Londonderry and Neptune statues was considered demolition, and the development proposed was over 1,000 square meters (Hunter 2010). English Heritage noted that the movement of the two listed statues represented another change in the life span of the Market Place which had consistently evolved throughout its existence. The relocation of the statues was not seen as a negative aspect of the Market Place plans.

2. Elvet Waterside

Another site, Elvet Waterside, has also engaged the attention of numerous stakeholders, particularly those from the student population in Durham. Currently, plans are on hold for the development of the site, but a review of the case demonstrates the importance of Durham's historic resources, including its World Heritage site.

Elvet Waterside is located along the River Wear, Figure 25, and is situated at the rear of Old Elvet, an area of Durham boasting a variety of listed buildings including ones owned by Durham University (Robinson 2010). In 1961 the Durham County Council reviewed the area for development. Records indicate that advertisements were published requesting land for "general town improvements" (DRO HTP 4/54); however, in 1962 a decision was made not to acquire the land.

The current area anticipated for development, Figures 26 and 27, includes land owned by Durham University and the Durham County Council. While most of the area is heavily residential, some land is used by the university and other organizations for sporting events throughout the year (DCC 08/00003/FPA). A planning application was presented in January 2008 for a mixed-use project with residences as well as leisure buildings. The

majority of the application was for new construction, and the local authority stated that its goal was to build something sensitive to the setting and conservation area (Herbert 2010).

The initial development process of the Elvet Waterside site involved a variety of stakeholders on account of its owners and position in the city. The area is not only located in the Durham City conservation area but also is in direct view of the World Heritage complex. Comments on the planning application were made by English Heritage, the City of Durham Trust, nature organizations, neighborhood groups, permanent residents, and students, and they ranged in topic from the type of development planned for the area

Figure 25 Elvet Waterside

Figure 26 Image of Elvet Waterside including the Durham World Heritage Site.

Figure 27 Elvet Waterside residential area.

-- noting that it was on a flood plain and in the sightline of the cathedral and castle -- to the impact on the lives of those who generally used the athletic portion of the property (DCC 08/00003/FPA).

A number of individuals cited the City of Durham Local Plan, noting that the area was an Area of High Landscape Value (AHLV) (City of Durham Trust 2008; DCC 08/00003/FPA). Civic and public organizations acknowledged the development's value but criticized the designs, stating they were not sensitive to the area and that elements such as height would create an adverse affect on the cultural heritage site. Students objected to the development because it would encroach on the sporting complex.

Information about the Elvet Waterside site was communicated through local newspapers and notices posted around the site itself. The local authority was also approached by members of the community regarding various aspects of the planned development. Consultations with the public, including an exhibition delivered by the developer of the project, were used to show the local residents what was planned (Herbert 2010).

The application for the development project was withdrawn in 2010 because of a downturn in the economy and challenges that emerged in achieving a plan agreed upon by all major stakeholders; however, the local authority and the university still plan to develop the site. It has been noted that true engagement with the residents will be needed going forward with the development (Robinson 2010). Local residents have been notified of the anticipated continuation of the scheme, and activities to include their input are being considered.

Swimming baths, also known as the public pools, Figure 28, are an additional feature of the Elvet Waterside development site. According to the Historic Environment Record for Durham County, the baths were constructed in the 1930s on the site of an earlier structure of the same purpose (Durham County Council 2010b).

English Heritage noted that the baths "contributed to the character and appearance of the conservation area" and suggested that they be retained. The swimming baths building is currently not listed and therefore its future will be determined by the local authority (DCC 08/00003/FPA; Tallentire 10 June 2010).

3. Former Ice Rink (Kascada Bowl)

The third site, the Ice Rink (Kascada Bowl), is the most complex of the three sites within this Durham study as its development was reviewed by not only the local planning authority but also by the Secretary of State for Communities and Local Government (DCC 05/00207/FPA). The Secretary has the power to request that a council direct a planning application to the government department (Hunter 2010). When an application is approached in this manner, it is dealt with by a public inquiry, and an inspector is employed to preside over it.

As it is the local government's statutory responsibility to seek the advice of English Heritage (EH) on projects involving historic properties, when the ice rink's applications for planning and conservation area consent were filed in 2003, EH became immediately involved as a major stakeholder (EH CHA/5197/0004). The Commission for Architecture and the Built Environment (CABE), also a recognized stakeholder, presented comments. Based on concerns by EH and CABE, it was determined that the applications be reevaluated, as the size and complexity of the project were felt to create an extreme impact on historic assets, placing at risk such places as the Durham City Conservation area, the World Heritage complex, and Crook Hall, a Grade I listed property positioned north of the former Ice Rink.

In 2005 new applications for planning and conservation area consent were filed for the Ice Rink site which included plans for residences as well as a leisure and heritage building along with a

Figure 28 Swimming Baths (public pool).

Figure 29 Elvet Waterside residential area and swimming baths (public pool).

public and cultural space (DCC 05/00207/FPA). The Ice Rink property, seen in Figures 30 and 31, was composed of a large building constructed in the 1940s for ice skating and a complex of unlisted yet historic buildings designated as Bishop's Mill. These latter structures "comprise a stone and clay pantile pre-1754 mill wheel chamber and adjacent accommodation, an adjoining early 19th century log wood mill in handmade brick and Welsh slate, and later associated buildings" (EH CHA/5197/0004). The site is located near one of the major transportation routes into the city and a recent modern development which includes a theater, library, and restaurants, Figure 33 (Durham City Vision 2007).

The later round of planning applications and conservation area consent applications contained plans which prompted strong objections by the public and some of the stakeholder organizations. English Heritage (EH CHA/5197/0004) expressed its own reservations during this phase as well. Despite objections, in December 2005 the City Council voted to approve the applications (DCC 05/00207/FPA). Then, in early 2006 the Secretary of State asked to review the applications and make a decision on the case. A public inquiry was held that summer. English Heritage, in response to the Secretary of State's comments concerning the situation, compiled a comprehensive framework of its position on the property's development.

For the public inquiry English Heritage established that the large-scale nature of the proposed construction would detract from the sight lines of the World Heritage site, the context of the Durham City conservation area, and Crook Hall. Furthermore, some of the structures anticipated for the final development were thought to be unsubstantial substitutes for the Bishop's Mill buildings being demolished. Although these buildings are unlisted, their historic significance and presence in the conservation area were noted (EH CHA/5197/0004).

Durham, England: Connecting Heritage with Revitalization Goals 75

Figure 30 Former Ice Rink

Figure 31 View of Bishop's Mill complex of buildings on Ice Rink site.

Figure 32 Side elevation of Bishop's Mill buildings on the Ice Rink site.

Figure 33 View of area surrounding Ice Rink site.

Proposals for development of the Ice Rink site also brought forth numerous comments and objections from other stakeholders. Unfortunately, the objections were not accessible for review.

Comments from other stakeholders have been noted in English Heritage documents. They included those from international heritage organizations such as UK/ICOMOS and highlight the significant effect the project would have on the "values" of the Durham Cathedral and Castle complex (EH CHA/5197/0004). One of the most vocal groups throughout the process, particularly in the public inquiry, was the civic organization the City of Durham Trust. The Trust works to inform the local community of issues impacting the historic architectural environment of Durham. An assessment of the Ice Rink (Kascada Bowl) site was presented by the City of Durham Trust at the public inquiry. The website of the organization notes that the mill buildings should be protected and that the anticipated buildings would not fit within the context of the site (City of Durham Trust, nd).

Following the review of proposals and statements by organizations such as English Heritage, including a report completed by the inspector appointed, the Secretary of State made the decision to refuse the Ice Rink applications. Within the past several years, the project has undergone a number of changes and design options in the quest to obtain a plan sensitive to the surrounding conservation area and the World Heritage site. The regional development agency One North East purchased the property for development by Durham City Vision (DCV). DCV subsequently published a new design brief and sought design and development partners. After the close of the organization in early 2012, final planning approvals were completed by the Durham County Council for the former Ice Rink and the site adjacent to it, Freeman's Reach. Construction work on the area began in late summer of 2013. The development will comprise new offices for the National Savings and Investments organization.

The Market Place, Elvet Waterside, and former Ice Rink (Kascada) sites illustrate the various voices that can be a part of the regeneration process and the challenges that can arise while incorporating conservation. The stakeholder analysis and influence map in the following section will show how issues may be resolved through the cultivation of specific relationships and the awareness of the true influences in a project.

INFLUENCE MAPPING & STAKEHOLDER ANALYSIS

In an analysis of the role of conservation in the urban renewal of Durham, several challenges emerged for those managing the process: 1) the cultivation of relationships among stakeholders, 2) communication, and 3) the integration of public value in decision making. The historic environment is an important factor for all connected to Durham, and in planning for the city it is a major element in the decisions made by its local government. Communication was found to be key in successfully moving the program through each of its phases.

An essential step in reducing communication challenges in a regeneration program is to identify all applicable stakeholders. Two concepts—stakeholder analysis and influence mapping--have been successfully implemented in the project management field to understand what stakeholders are intrinsic to a project and to ensure that all are included appropriately. These concepts also help in determining areas where more communication between stakeholders should occur. This section will illustrate how the strategies can be completed using the Durham project as an example and depicting those involved and their relationships with each other.

The influence map, shown in Figures 34 and 35, presents a comprehensive view of the stakeholders pertinent to the three sites reviewed. The stakeholder analysis and influence map are interrelated as the research of the stakeholders contributes to the creation of the influence map. While the map presents a picture of how each stakeholder influences each other, it also serves as a guide to predicting where future emphasis should be placed. After identifying the stakeholders, they were divided into primary and secondary groups and illustrated in diagrams, Figures 36 and 37. The former includes those whose interest in the project was vital to its outcome. The latter group consists of organizations or individuals who held some influence on the program or would be affected by it in some way. The diagram depicts stakeholders uncovered through research of the project, whether through a review of the program's master plan, through the media, or through interviews with stakeholders. In addition to these stakeholders, many others were located that would potentially be affected by the program, but it was decided to include only those most pertinent to the three cases reviewed in this study.

The United Kingdom census records most recent at the time of the initial study show the city of Durham with a population of 42,939, with approximately one-third being post-secondary-aged (college-aged in USA) students (Office for National Statistics 2004). The data collected pertaining to the stakeholders was included in two tables, Tables 1 and 2. They are broken down by stakeholder and highlighted according to their "importance to the project," "key interests," and "participation" (Mayers 2005). From this an analysis can begin of the ways to mitigate challenges and ensure a positive outcome for the program, particularly for the conservation of the historic environment of Durham. The stakeholders included in the tables are those from the primary group as they provide a solid basis for illustrating the connections among the stakeholders and give a comprehensive picture of the case study.

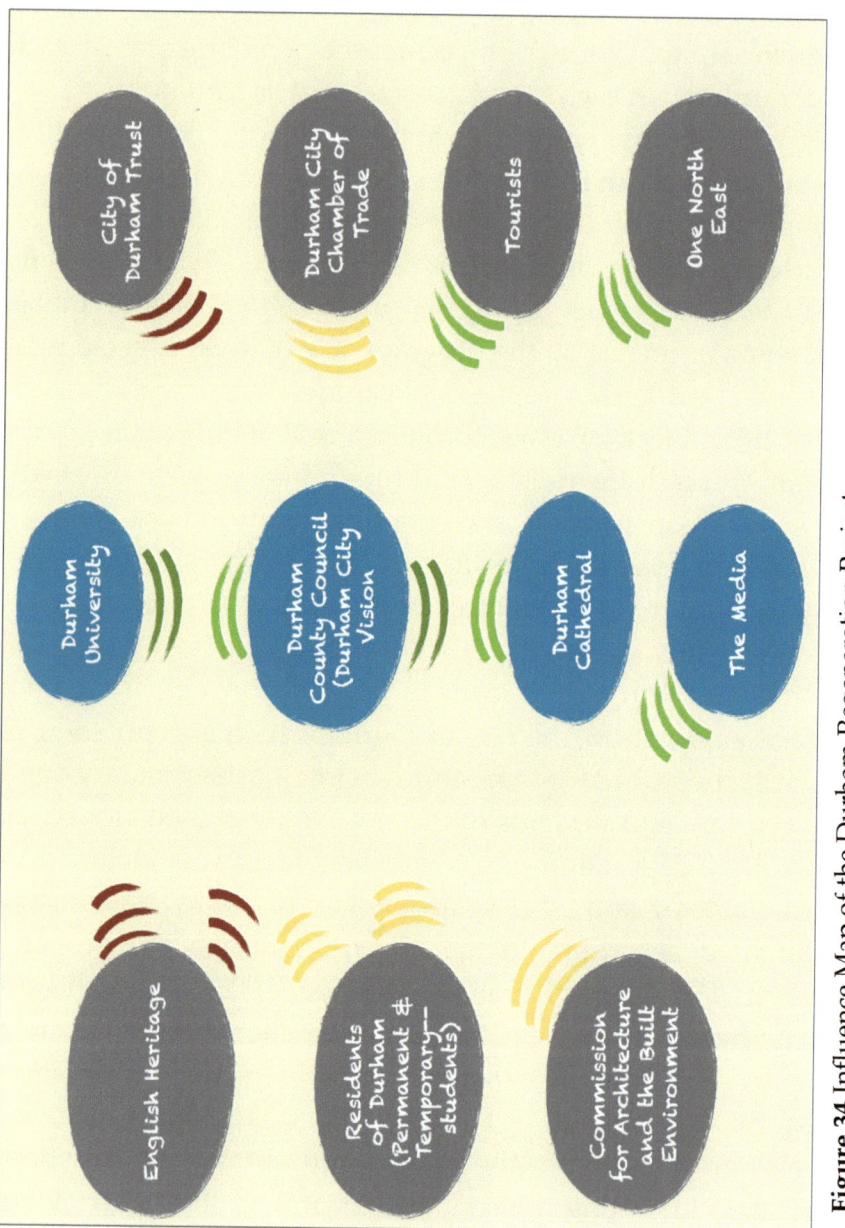

Figure 34 Influence Map of the Durham Regeneration Project

Figure 35 A second view of the Influence Map of the Regeneration program in Durham highlighting additional stakeholders.

Figure 36 A view of the primary stakeholders in the Durham regeneration program.

Figure 37 A view of the secondary stakeholders in the Durham regeneration program.

STAKEHOLDERS	KEY INTERESTS	IMPORTANCE TO PROJECT	PARTICIPATION
PRIMARY			
Durham County Council (Durham City Vision--DCV)	•Effectively protecting city's architectural heritage through partnership with heritage bodies, specialists and residents •Gaining opinions of residents on redevelopment designs	•High •Decision makers who provide leadership in regeneration process.	•Council completed reviews of the planning/listed building/conservation area consent applications for Market Place, Elvet Waterside and Ice Rink (Kascada Bowl) •DCV organised consultations with public on Market Place
Durham Cathedral	•Protection and care of the cathedral and its buildings •Setting of the World Heritage site and cathedral	•High •Large landowner: Durham Cathedral and its structures	•Engaged in consultations on the flood lighting scheme for the World Heritage site and feasibility study for visitor facilities
Durham University	•Managing and protecting the university's buildings •Setting of the World Heritage site	•High •A major landowner in the city: co-owner of Elvet Waterside property and owner of 21 listed buildings at World Heritage site, including Durham Castle.	•Conducted consultations with residents at Elvet Waterside •Engaged in consultations on the flood lighting scheme for the World Heritage site and feasibility study for visitor facilities
City of Durham Trust	•Informing the public on planning matters	•High •Opinions and actions impact the outcome of the regeneration efforts.	•Coordinated the Market Place petition •Presented assessment of Ice Rink plans for Secretary of State review
English Heritage	•Early involvement with development discussions •Developing a partnership with local government for smooth project delivery •Consultation on project design briefs	•High •Will engage in statutory consultation on projects	•Provided comments on Market Place, Elvet Waterside and ice rink (Kascada Bowl) sites •Provided report on Ice Rink (Kascada Bowl) particulars for Secretary of State review
Developers	•Producing a high quality redevelopment that is satisfactory for all stakeholders. •Continued dialogue with stakeholders throughout the project conception stage.	•High •Will present designs for locations included in the regeneration masterplan	•Created designs for the redevelopment of the Market Place, Elvet Waterside and the Ice Rink (Kascada Bowl) •Consulted with residents at Elvet Waterside

Table 1 Illustration of Primary stakeholders seen in the Market Place, Elvet Waterside and Ice Rink (Kascada Bowl) sites (Stakeholder Analysis Table © James Mayers)

STAKEHOLDERS	KEY INTERESTS	IMPORTANCE TO PROJECT	PARTICIPATION
PRIMARY			
One North East	•Economic development of the city. •Sustainability through the regeneration process.	•High •Provides funding for regeneration efforts in Durham.	•Purchased Ice Rink property for redevelopment by Durham City Vision •Provided funds for Market Place grant scheme.
Residents of Durham (Permanent and temporary -- students)	•Preserving the historic character and feel of the city •Understanding the scope of the regeneration organiser and masterplan	•High •Opinions and actions impact the outcome of the regeneration efforts.	•Market Place consultations, surveys and exhibition •Market Place petition •Contributed comments regarding Market Place, Elvet Waterside and Ice Rink (Kascada Bowl) design plans

Table 2 Illustration of Primary stakeholders seen in the Market Place, Elvet Waterside and Ice Rink (Kascada Bowl) sites (Stakeholder Analysis Table © *James Mayers*)

To pinpoint the location of major influences, an influence map of the three sites was created which revealed influences not generally perceived by stakeholders. The map is based on the major stakeholders uncovered for each case and includes those groups or organizations noted as vocal or decision-making and predominant throughout the interview and literature review phases of research.

Those with larger and bolder arcs radiating from them, such as English Heritage and the local community, had a greater influence due to the results of their comments on the work planned for the sites. The width of the arcs and their direction illustrate the nature of the influence, with the wider arcs depicting greater influence. Wider arcs depict greater influence, and the color signifies the type; for example, amber encourages caution, red sometimes stops a process, and green represents fluidity of actions and communication between the organization or group and other stakeholders. The results of this technique and its future use will be discussed in the following chapter.

THE ASSESSMENT OF PUBLIC VALUE

Public value is an essential aspect of any regeneration project, and an ongoing assessment of how and in what capacity it is being delivered is advised. As stated in the opening chapter, public value is embracing the opinions of the public as well as educating the public on aspects of planning to equip them in participating in the process (Clark 2006a). Within this case study on Durham, steps were taken by the local authority to provide public value to the city's residents, particularly regarding plans for heritage in the city. Public interactions initiated by the major stakeholders -- Durham County Council and its partnering organization Durham City Vision along with Durham University -- will be described here, and further conclusions will be provided in the following chapter.

Scholars have noted two areas within the assessment of public value by a decision maker: 1) "capacity of an organisation" for generating public value and 2) "the quantification of responsiveness" to the activities completed by the public (Blaug, Horner and Kekhi 2006). Both points illustrate an organization's efforts to use the opinions and thoughts of the public to educate them in making appropriate decisions regarding heritage. The Durham case study included varying amounts of details on the public engagement related to each site. The Market Place was the most comprehensive of the three projects. As mentioned above, several consultations were hosted as part of the Market Place design plans. These were initiated by a consultant at various points throughout a two-year period, incorporating the participation of a variety of stakeholders which included public officials and individuals from Durham University, local businesses, business trade organizations, and a local school (Your Shout Communications 2009).

Feedback from the local community was obtained through surveys made available at many of the consultation events. Overall, the goal of these periods of public engagement was to give the public an opportunity to gain an understanding of what was envisioned for the design of the Market Place. The meetings were carefully organized to achieve this goal. For example, during the preliminary period the reception of the project and initial design thoughts were assessed. The middle period was dedicated to guiding the local community, including its student and visitor population, through the public and informal exhibitions of the designs (Your Shout Communications 2009).

These types of public interactions included "deliberative engagements" (opportunities were constructed to speak with the public), "consultations" (the local community was questioned about their opinions of the designs), "user participation," and "consumer feedback..." which were solicited through surveys (Blaug, Horner and Kekhi 2006; Your Shout Communications 2009). These interactions demonstrated "responsiveness" by the Durham County Council and Durham City Vision to the preferences of the community regarding the design of the Market Place (Blaug, Horner and Kekhi 2006). They are seen as essential to producing public value.

It was found that consultations were completed prior to the publication of the regeneration plan which focused the local authority's general work on the Market Place (Hurlow 2010). These types of public engagements -- "ongoing evaluation" and "educational initiatives" -- have been noted to complete the process of working to provide public value (Blaug, Horner and Kekhi 2006). This process of assessing public value allows the decision maker to view opportunities where engagement with the public can be improved. When this is completed before the start, a plan can be developed, and during the program any changes that need to be completed may be applied per the results of initial activities.

The preliminary review of the planning policies and conservation planning activities in Durham's history provided a foundation for understanding the present regeneration program. The information obtained through the investigation of the three sites provided areas in which to evaluate the influence of conservation and uncover how aspects of the field such as *significance* and *values* are represented. The process of completing the stakeholder analysis and influence map and obtaining results from both also contributes to an understanding of what may be completed going forward, both on pending cases and those to be initiated in the near future.

...Write down the vision clearly on tablets, so that even a runner can read it.

Habakkuk 2:2 NIV

When we build, let us think that we build forever. Let it not be for present delight nor for our use alone. Let it be such work as our descendants will look upon with praise and thanksgiving in their hearts.
--John Ruskin, Artist, Art Critic, Patron of the Arts & Philanthropist

5 Emerging Themes

An investigation of Durham's regeneration program, specifically the Market Place, Elvet Waterside, and the former Ice Rink (Kascada), has uncovered a few pertinent themes common to all three projects: 1) authenticity and the relevance of new design as it relates to the historic character of the conservation area, 2) the importance of the setting of the Durham World Heritage site, and 3) the prominent role communication plays in delivering projects such as these while incorporating a wide range of stakeholders.

According to authors Feilden and Jokilehto (1998), one of the keys to successful outcomes of projects in regeneration programs such as that of County Durham is balancing the needs of conservation and development. Another key the authors observed is developing a true sense of the historic fabric of a town. Because Durham's citizens place a high value on maintaining their city's historic fabric, this was reflected and established in the program's master plan (Durham City Vision 2007).

During the public inquiry period, comments were delivered by public organizations and the local community. The historic environment and its inherent values were the main topics of the comments delivered. The concerns noted that in each of the above sites retaining these values did not appear to be part of the core focus of the Durham County Council. The unlisted swimming baths at Elvet Waterside and Bishop's Mill at the Ice Rink site were presented as examples of this. The public comments also questioned the validity of the plans for the conservation area and their impact on the World Heritage site pervaded the collective assessments by stakeholders. From this evidence it appears that a tool of conservation planning discussed frequently--the conservation area character appraisal-- would be a vital aid in helping to focus development work and establish consensus between the public and the local government (English Heritage 2006a; 2006b). The character appraisal may also lead to determining what needs in the city could be filled by the successful retention or adaptive reuse of the unlisted structures at the locations.

A conservation area character appraisal for the city of Durham is currently being developed. The current activities there, however, illustrate the vital and immediate need for the appraisal. It is an element that may be used in the management of the historic environment to conserve those aspects that define the significance of a place and aid the production of sensitive development plans (English Heritage 2006a). The completion of a conservation area character appraisal will consolidate information on the various building phases seen throughout the historical periods in Durham. It will also include maps and images showing the historical development of the area and its significant historic places.

The planning documents such as the Local Plan, used as part of the Local Development Framework, also include policies relating to the characteristics of Durham's historic architecture. A concise explanation is given of the type of modern design that is expected, but the nature of the plan does not allow for comprehensively addressing the needs for the area and the existing historic resources that will be affected should development take place (Durham City Council, nd). To address this need, the stakeholder analysis and the influence map is recommended. Through those processes, one can take an expansive and holistic view of the project to see where additional work can be completed to achieve the goals noted in an appraisal.

Scholars such as Feilden and Jokilehto (1998) support the concept of conservation area character appraisals. They note that it would be valuable to evaluate the past causes of development or decline in various periods and to investigate how earlier town plans have been implemented and the range of historic fabric that exists from previous phases. They argue that the ultimate objective will be for towns to use the information as part of a master plan to guide decisions and development so the values of the urban area are retained and development does not create negative effects.

Comments made by stakeholders during the evaluation of Durham's sites included references to the concepts of values and authenticity. Statements surrounding the appropriate use of materials for the Market Place and the impact of new construction both at Elvet Waterside and the former Ice Rink (Kascada) in relation to the Durham Cathedral and Castle complex reflect the emerging use of these concepts in the context of town planning. Various authors have discussed the influence of authenticity as it is conveyed through the Nara document and the Venice Charter. The challenges noted, such as the potentially negative impact when "authentic community uses" (the way in which a community has used an area historically, for example, the traditional use of a market place as a place of gathering) and connections with historic places are disrupted, appear relevant for Durham (Otero-Pailos, Gaiger and West

2010). The Market Place has undergone multiple phases of development, Elvet Waterside has continued for many years to be an area of homes and sports complexes, and the Ice Rink has significant links to the city's recent and medieval past. The major focus of the town is the World Heritage site which has intense significance locally and internationally. The local community and the heritage professionals have associated values with these evolutions, making their preservation a high priority.

Another reoccurring theme in all three cases is the implication of a buffer zone. The Durham World Heritage site does not currently have one although there have been discussions on the topic per the coordinator of the site, and it is under review (El-Rashidi 2010). It has been agreed, however, to extend the current boundaries of the site to encompass the river banks beneath it. Considering Durham's historic significance, development within the boundaries of the town would need to be carefully executed. Yet it appears that comments generated by one of the main stakeholders, English Heritage, encourage creation of a buffer zone as the organization consistently refers to the need to protect the setting around the World Heritage site in their assessments. Although buffer zones are not required for World Heritage sites, they are recommended to protect the "Outstanding Universal Value" of the property (UNESCO World Heritage Centre 2010).

The study of the three sites revealed that the residents of Durham were very vocal about the changes that were planned for the city. While the local authority noted this as a challenge in completing development, it appeared that the residents were not objecting simply to change but to the effects they perceived the new construction would have on the values they associated with the town, for example, its historic character and the residents' long experience with the sites. These types of values are illustrated by the classifications presented by scholars and organizations such as Riegl and

English Heritage. Terms such as "historic" and "use value" demonstrate the importance of the age of some of the areas and length of time that they have been utilized. Yet praise received from the local residents, including those with disabilities, on the change of the landscape of the Market Place illustrates a benefit of consultation. This Market Place example shows that the decision maker's efforts to connect with local citizens were successful, increasing residents' engagement with the project instead of turning them away. It also appears that the efforts by the decision makers are leading towards meeting requirements of the Disability Discrimination Act (DDA) 2005 which mandates greater access for the disabled population.

Scholar Jane Grenville (2007) discusses how people may react when their environment changes in an unexpected or drastic way. She summarizes Anthony Giddens' (1991) theory of "ontological security" -- the constructed environment people tend to exist in socially that aids them in functioning -- to illustrate the influence of change on individuals within the "built environment." Grenville argues that this can be seen in various ways in society, sometimes in a dramatic manner when people attempt to recreate their previous sense of security that has somehow been lost. This can be seen in Durham in the sometimes negative reactions of the residential and non-profit sector stakeholder groups to choices made regarding development.

STAKEHOLDER ANALYSIS AND INFLUENCE MAP

The stakeholder analysis and influence map illustrate the nature of the stakeholders involved in Durham's regeneration process and their role in its outcome. The analysis provided visuals, exhibited through the division of primary and secondary stakeholders, to relate the variety of participation levels. The influence map showed how and to what degree each group made an impact on the other

Figure 38 View of the finished Market Place. (© *Durham County Council/Durham City Vision*)

in the program. It has been argued that until a critical view is taken of a project crucial participants may be overlooked (Mind Tools 2010). As the influence map points out, truly influential stakeholders in the three projects under review were not apparent during the initial evaluation.

Specifically, a perusal of the influence map showed that English Heritage, the organization providing statutory advice on all three projects, was a stakeholder that had the ability to influence the completion of the activities planned. The local community and the civic organization City of Durham Trust also held more influence than was initially perceived by those involved. In comments by Durham residents, concerns were expressed that their opinions would be of low importance to decision makers, but this was not found to be the case. The design of the Market Place included some adaptations due to the consultations with the public, and it was noted that City of Durham Trust held a great deal of weight on the development outcome of the Ice Rink site (EH CHA/5197/0004).

Together, both tools revealed areas where decision makers needed to increase their efforts to build relationships with other stakeholders. Information gathered on each of the stakeholders in the analysis can be used to understand their position and to focus engagement efforts.

In the final determination of the Ice Rink, however, the mill buildings were authorized to be demolished and are currently being cleared to be replaced by an Archimedes screw hydroelectric power system, part of the sustainable energy initiative for the site. The removal of the medieval structures was a pivotal decision and will have an effect on subsequent development steps owing to the precedence this has set. The Durham City Trust stated that an interpretation board will be installed to describe the historic structures previously situated on the property.

A revised master plan has recently been created to "complement existing council guidance and documents, including the emerging County Durham Plan" (Durham County Council 2013). The document further describes how Durham is positioned through its heritage, culture, and economic benefits to lead the surrounding county in a successful regeneration effort. One of the main areas stated to be addressed by the regeneration program was tourism--more specifically, how to enhance the visitor experience and attract more visitors to the city. In this vein a visitor's center was constructed and opened in 2011 (Figures 39-41). This new center has drawn in approximately 100,000 individuals each year since its opening (El-Rashidi 2013). Activities hosted at the property have included a stone masonry workshop, art exhibitions, lectures, and small concerts.

Figure 39 Exterior of the Durham World Heritage Site Visitors Centre. (© *Durham World Heritage Site/Andrew Heptinstall*)

Figure 40 Interior of the Durham World Heritage Site Visitors Centre.
(© *Durham World Heritage Site/Andrew Heptinstall*)

Figure 41 An event at the Durham World Heritage Site Visitors Centre.
(© *Durham World Heritage Site/Andrew Heptinstall*)

The themes of authenticity and values in conservation planning, the importance of public engagement to deliver public value, and the utilization of strategic tools of stakeholder analysis and influence mapping reflect a holistic view of the research results of the Durham sites. They offer valid areas of investigation in the attempt to create successful results for each of the projects.

Let us not become weary in doing good, for at the proper time we will reap a harvest if we do not give up.

Galatians 6:9 NIV

It's not good because it's old, it's old because it's good.
--Anonymous

6 The Global Revitalization Landscape: A Further Look

Historic Preservation, or conservation planning, is a process that takes place throughout the world, and its role is seen at varying levels. In some instances the revitalization of historic areas is used to create more cohesion between a community's stakeholders. Other programs are focused more on using historic places to increase the economic situation of an area. Although the specific goals may differ slightly in each case, reviewing the treatment of historic places within a revitalization project offers a chance to learn and to improve other programs in the future. The two additional international cases presented in this chapter provide further opportunity to review solutions to challenges in programs similar to those of Durham as well as to show the varied approaches to stakeholder engagement and the benefits of a preservation-focused project in which the surrounding community is included.

BASTROP, LOUISIANA (UNITED STATES)

Preservation planning in the USA has been cultivated through the development of historic resource surveys, the creation and use of preservation plans for cities and communities, and the development of governance bodies such as historic preservation commissions. The national authoritative document presiding over the field is the National Historic Preservation Act of 1966 (NHPA 1966). It established a structure for work in the field throughout the country. Connected to this policy was the creation of the "Secretary of the Interior's Standards for the Treatment of Historic Properties" (National Park Service, nd). These documents are intended for those who care for historic structures and are particularly important within revitalization programs.

The first program is located in Bastrop, Louisiana, in the southern region of the United States. A town of approximately 12,000 residents, Bastrop is positioned in Morehouse Parish in the northern portion of the state, Figure 42. The area of Bastrop was first settled in 1796 by Dutch nobleman Felipe Enrique Neri, Baron de Bastrop, later by Colonel Abraham Morehouse from Kentucky. Bastrop was incorporated in 1852 (City of Bastrop Louisiana 2007).

The town experienced a downturn in its economy in 2008 through the closing of its paper mill, the International Paper Company, which employed a large number of the city's residents. In response to the city's decline, a ten-year redevelopment plan was completed to guide planning (King 2010).

The revitalization that took place in Bastrop began in 2000 when the state's Historic Preservation division allocated funds to the City of Bastrop Main Street program. Main Street then allocated the funds for various economic development activities. The Main Street program is part of a national network under the auspices of

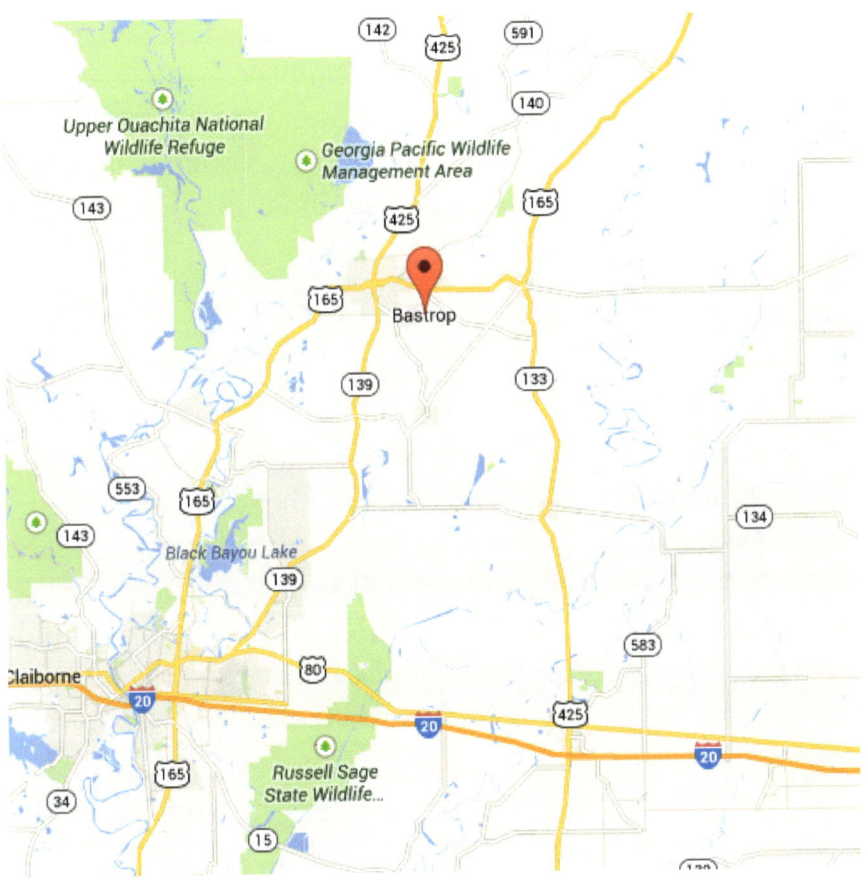

Figure 42 Bastrop, Louisiana. (Map Data © 2014 Google)

the National Main Street Center. The center developed a "four-point approach" to regenerating an area, encompassing "organization," "promotion," "design," and "economic restructuring" (National Trust for Historic Preservation 2009).

The National Main Street Center works with state governments but typically with local non-profits to provide ideas, resources, and support to facilitate the unique approach. These bodies are usually the Main Street organizations functioning within the non-profit sector for small- to medium-size towns. The focus of the program involves mobilizing the entire local community, using existing resources, local leaders, and a number of volunteers to increase the feasibility of projects that are planned. Attention is placed on the use of "heritage," including historic architecture, in efforts to improve the economic climate in an area (National Trust for Historic Preservation 2009). This approach has also been translated to other countries such as Australia, Canada, and Japan (Adkins 2010).

In the case of Bastrop, the monies provided by the state government were matched at the local level by the city and designated for the restoration of the exteriors of businesses positioned on the perimeter of the town's core area, the courthouse square. The businesses are situated in a historic district which imposes certain requirements regulated by the Bastrop Historic District Commission (Alford-Olive 2010; Vereen 2010). The commission governs building details such as signage, exterior landscaping such as fencing and color changes, and exists to retain the historical integrity of the buildings.

The city currently has one historic district, Figure 43, and encompasses the portion of the city that has great historic significance and architectural value for its residents. Within the first five years of the Main Street program, 24 properties were restored. The stakeholders included the City of Bastrop Main Street board and respective committees: the Bastrop Chamber of Commerce (which acted as the economic development committee) and the Morehouse Economic Development Corporation.

One of the main challenges in the program was initiating the process. Previously, many of the buildings around the square had "aluminum slip covers" that covered the historic fabric of the structures, Figure 44. Local community members felt the removal of the metal casing would not preserve the character of the city. The City of Bastrop Main Street's board members collectively worked to

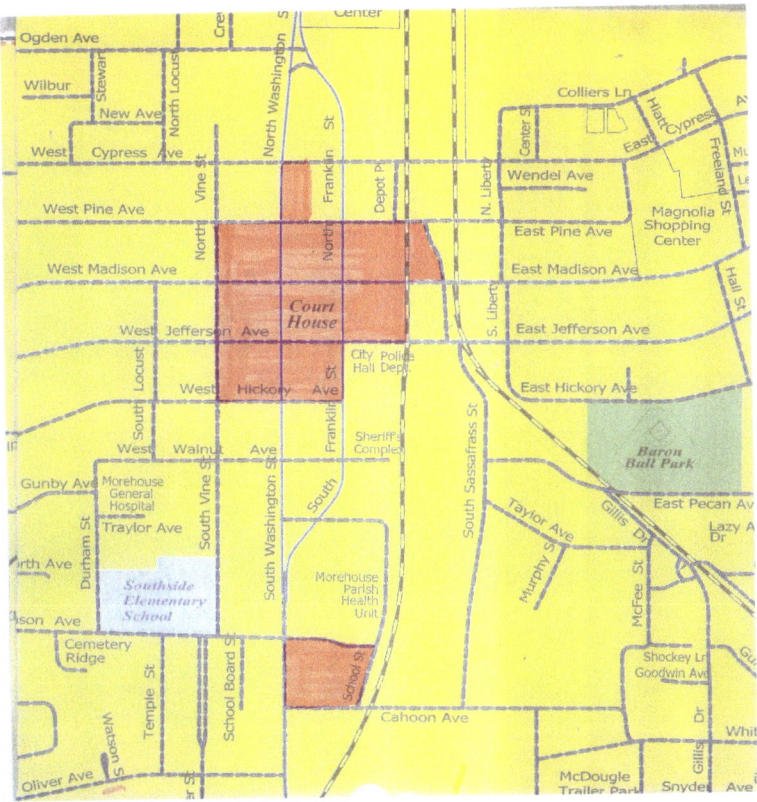

Figure 43 The downtown historic district in Bastrop, Louisiana.
(© Bastrop Main Street)

evaluate the problem and found that the local community was not completely aware of what was planned. Partnerships were then developed with institutions such as the Louisiana State University School of Architecture to develop a community design charrette. This type of event worked to convey the benefits of the revitalization program as well as the immediate plans for the restoration of the commercial buildings.

Visual displays, including renderings by a City of Bastrop Main Street board member, were presented to depict what the structures looked like in the past and what they could look like in the future. These images, Figures 45-48, illustrated the goals of the

Figure 44 The downtown historic district in Bastrop, Louisiana.
(© Bastrop Main Street)

Figure 45 A historic postcard of downtown Bastrop, Louisiana.
(© Bastrop Main Street)

program and served to engage more of the local community. Following these activities the benefit of enhancing the buildings was seen more clearly, leading to a successful regeneration of the area, Figures 49-50. Some successful business owners experienced an

Figure 46 Renderings completed for proposed restoration of buildings in the historic district of Bastrop, Louisiana. (© Larry James)

increase in patronage after the completion of the restoration project (Arnett 2010).

The Bastrop Main Street program may be seen as a successful project, particularly in the area of communication. The program's decision maker worked to convey the goals and vision to the stakeholders and engage them within the process. Currently, the organization is continuing its quest to promote the restoration of other buildings in the historic district and increase the economic vitality of the city. One of the issues foreseen in the future for cities and towns like Bastrop is the overwhelming challenge of restoring historic buildings for public use. Although this is not seen as a major problem in Bastrop, it was argued that this puts a great deal of pressure on local governments who are working within limited budgets (King 2010). A project undertaken to offset budgetary constraints was the adaptive reuse of a local historic high school structure into apartments for retirees (Helbling 5 June 2010). This project, also part of the city's historic district, was completed in 2011.

The Tudor Revival Structure, Figures 51-53, is a major landmark in the town and was listed on the National Register for Historic Places in 2002. Its restoration was a major feat and included strong sustainability efforts. Journalist Conan Cheong noted that "[The] largest residential solar system in all of Louisiana [was installed] on the building's spacious roof—430 solar panels that generate up to 106 kilowatts of power daily." The project was an encouraging success to those participating in it, and the town has seen follow-up development work as well. An affordable housing development was later created a short distance from the historic high school restoration project and has added to the revitalization momentum. Although the homes are contemporary, the architects employed a traditional design to harmonize with the historic properties surrounding the subdivision.

Figure 47 Renderings completed for proposed restoration of buildings in the historic district of Bastrop, Louisiana. (© *Larry James*)

Partnerships have continued to be cultivated as the city's Main Street organization frequently works with the main library in the Parish, the Visitor's Center, and the town's historic theater. The organization sponsors cultural events with a historic theme such as high teas and contemporary films in a historic setting. One of the challenges, however, that has surfaced for the town is the increase of derelict commercial and residential historic properties. Some structures outside the town's historic district have reached such extreme states of disrepair that they have been demolished. A large number are heir properties with a number of individuals holding claim to the land but with no one to initiate restoration work. This has put a strain on city planning and preservation initiatives.

Two of the historic neighborhoods near Bastrop's city center have a mixture of early 20th-century to mid-century modern dwellings in varying states of repair. The development of an additional historic district is being discussed for these buildings to provide greater protection for their historic resources. Another challenge is that many owners have an interest but lack the necessary monetary resources to restore their properties. By using the tools outlined previously, the stakeholder analysis and influence map, possible solutions to this may be attained.

    The stakeholder group of tourists is seen to exert some influence on the revitalization activities of the town, but many are from the immediately surrounding area, and some are from the largest municipality near the city, Monroe. This illustrates an area of opportunity outside Bastrop's central downtown district to alleviate the funding gap for revitalization. Establishing events that can draw in a diverse group of people, even from bordering states will increase economic activity, and the funds can then be invested into the historic structures that stand as examples not only of the city's heritage but also of architecture throughout the country.

Figure 48 Renderings completed for proposed restoration of buildings in the historic district of Bastrop, Louisiana. (© Larry James)

Figure 49 Businesses after the Bastrop courthouse square restoration project. (© *Bastrop Main Street*)

Figure 50 Businesses after the Bastrop courthouse square restoration project. (© *Bastrop Main Street*)

Figure 51 Front facade of the Bastrop historic highschool.

Figure 52 Side view of the Bastrop historic highschool project.

Figure 53 The Bastrop historic highschool project.

In discussions with property owners, comments have surfaced that the area appears to be worsening instead of improving. As positive change occurs, the restoration of the neighborhoods will impact tourism, encouraging more individuals to visit the city while increasing the morale of local residents as well. Bastrop has made progress since the economic downturn of 2008. Through each of the town's restoration projects, another building is added, exemplifying what tenacity and vision can accomplish. Through budget restraints and population changes, the city has continued to showcase its historic resources and strive for additional opportunities to increase its success.

JAFFA (YAFO), ISRAEL

The second international site is Jaffa (Yafo in Hebrew), Israel. The city joined its northern neighbor Tel Aviv in 1950, creating the metropolitan area of Tel Aviv-Yafo (Encyclopedia Britannica Online 2010). It is located in the northwest portion of Israel along the Mediterranean Sea, Figures 58 and 59. The area has an expansive

Figure 54 A photograph of one of the mid-century residential properties in Bastrop, Louisiana prior to its restoration.

Figure 55 The mid-century property after its restoration (Historic Preservation specialist Lydia Atubeh).

Figure 56 An interior photo of the mid-century property in Bastrop, Louisiana prior to its restoration.

Figure 57 An interior photo of the property after its restoration (Historic Preservation specialist Lydia Atubeh).

The Global Revitalization Landscape: A Further Look   115

Figure 58 Jaffa, Israel. (© *Google*)

Figure 59 An aerial view of Jaffa, Israel. (© *Society for the Preservation of Israel Heritage Sites*)

Figure 60 A historic photograph of the Jaffa clock tower.
(© *Society for the Preservation of Israel Heritage Sites*)

Figure 61 1917 photograph of Jaffa's town hall. (© *Society for the Preservation of Israel Heritage Sites*)

Figure 62 Jaffa's Town hall prior to the regeneration project.
(© *Society for the Preservation of Israel Heritage Sites*)

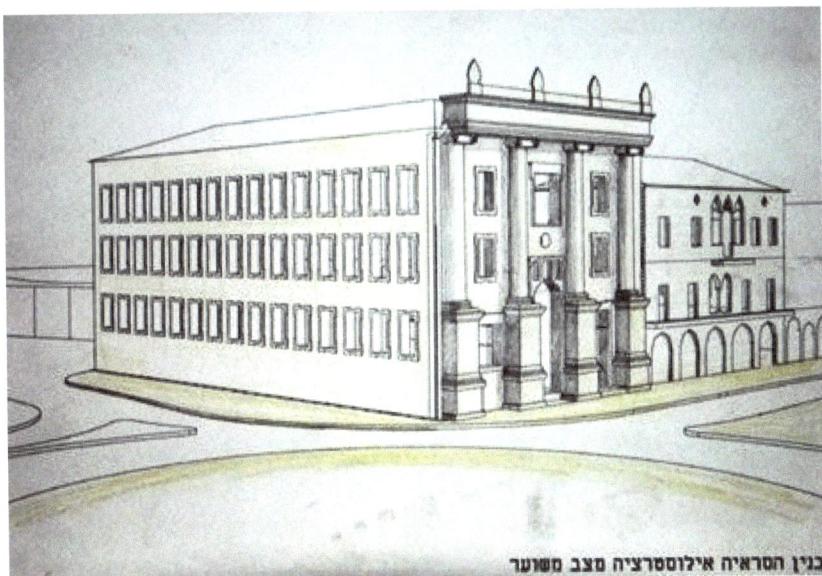

Figure 63 First rendering illustrating possible design of Jaffa's old town hall. (© *Society for the Preservation of Israel Heritage Sites*)

Figure 64 Second rendering of the possible design of Jaffa's old town hall. (© *Society for the Preservation of Israel Heritage Sites*)

Figure 65 Rear view of the second rendering of a possible design of Jaffa's old town hall. (© *Society for the Preservation of Israel Heritage Sites*)

The Global Revitalization Landscape: A Further Look 119

Figure 66 Side view of the remaining structure of Jaffa's old town hall after regeneration.

Figure 67 Front facade view of Jaffa's old town hall and its adjoining building after the regeneration project.

120 *Rebuilding A Jewel: Successful Strategies for Revitalizing Historic Places*

Figure 68 Jaffa's old town hall, clock tower and surrounding area after regeneration.

Figure 69 The Jaffa clock tower after the regeneration project.

Figure 70 View of historic Jaffa storefronts prior to restoration.

history as it was mentioned in connection with major individuals and events in the Bible (LeBor 8 May 2008). One of its significant features was the Old Jaffa port, at one time the second largest port in the country, but it was closed in 1965 (Encyclopaedia Britannica Online 2010). The historic area around the site was recently revitalized (Zevi 2010).

According to the country's last census which was conducted by the Central Bureau of Statistics in 2008, Tel Aviv-Yafo had a population of 392,500. This does not effectively represent the number of individuals in Jaffa as the town is now considered to be a suburb of Tel Aviv, a much larger city. The numbers do, however, provide a sense of the large number of individuals who influence the area. Various cultural groups may be seen in the locale, including Arabs and Jews (Tuchler 2010).

Conservation planning in Israel is typically administered at the local government level. In Tel Aviv-Yafo the municipality has made a list of all its buildings of historical value. When buildings

Figure 71 View of Jaffa businesses after the regeneration program.

Figure 72 Additional view of Jaffa businesses after the regeneration program.

Figure 73 An aerial view of the proposed W Hotel.
(© *Scherf Communications*)

Figure 74 A rendering of the poolside view of the W Hotel in Jaffa, Israel. (© *Scherf Communications*)

Figure 75 An interior view of the historic French hospital portion of the new W Hotel in Jaffa, Israel. (© *Scherf Communications*)

are publicly owned—and approximately one-quarter of the buildings are owned by the city--plans are developed to preserve them

(Alfasi and Fabian 2009; Zevi 2010). Currently, Israel does not have a nationwide conservation policy, but one is being developed. Because of the lack of a national plan for conservation, one challenge that has been noted is encouraging residents to maintain their properties. The country does have a number of prominent heritage organizations and conservation professionals who are working to illustrate the positive effect of regeneration. Within Tel Aviv-Yafo these professional, non-profit, and non-governmental groups are working with the municipality to bring about a change in the attitudes of the public towards preserving historic properties.

Jaffa's revitalization program began in 1998. The improvements have taken place within public spaces and buildings around the area's historic clock tower, Figure 60, as well as in areas near this commercial part of the town. The project involved a number of stakeholders including the conservation architect who managed the restoration of the various historic structures, Eyal Ziv, the Society for Preservation of Israel Heritage Sites (a non-governmental organization), the municipality, and local business owners and residents.

Several challenges were encountered within the project. One of the first was engaging the support of the local community and government. It was thought by many that the program was too difficult and would not succeed. The municipality was hesitant to provide funds and very cautious about beginning the regeneration. Some of the stakeholders working together to produce the project, particularly the conservation architect, demonstrated to officials how the process could create more of a sense of community in Tel Aviv-Yafo. This was done by inviting them to travel through the area to show them what could be done and the benefits (Tuchler 2010).

Another issue involved the final design for Jaffa's town hall, also known as the Saria building, pictured in Figures 61 and 62.

Some wanted to completely reconstruct the building while others felt that not enough was known of its history to provide an accurate restoration. This was a major factor as the lead architect wanted the projects to be as true to the history of the area as possible (BBC News 2008). Renderings were completed to illustrate the options for the structure, depicted in Figures 63-65. After some time the clock tower as well as the Saria building were restored, Figures 66-69. This was encouraging to those in the locale and increased their confidence in the project (BBC News 2008).

One of the other issues to emerge within the project involved the restoration of the exterior portions of the businesses surrounding the clock tower. Many of the store owners valued their unique shop facades and wanted to retain them. The regeneration leaders worked to show the owners the historic character of the shops and the importance of using signage that fit the scale and style of the structures. After working to communicate with proprietors, the initiators were able to demonstrate the need to protect and care for the historic architecture and complete the restoration of the buildings, pictured in Figures 70-72.

The Jaffa revitalization project has also included investment by luxury hospitality company Starwood Hotels & Resorts Worldwide Inc. The company has obtained the 19th-century historic French Hospital in Jaffa as the location for the first W Hotel brand in Israel. Construction is planned to include hotel rooms, a restaurant, and bar area which will be positioned within the historic structure, Figures 73-75. The development will also include permanent residences that will be constructed next to the historic property.

Planning for the rehabilitation of the historic French Hospital was noted to have taken several years owing to the nature of the project and discussions with heritage groups. Reut Gilady (2013), from Scherf Communications (public relations contact for the hotel), states that the process of melding both the new "next to the old" brought forth challenges in the design, but these were surmountable. The company noted that the "architectural features-from the original buildings and two thousand year old foundations uncovered during the construction [will be] carefully integrated into the public space designs." Full details on how the heritage of the site will be assimilated into the hotel's activities for its guests have not been confirmed. Gilady noted, however, that "the history of the place will be integrated into the project, such as [displaying] the archaeological findings in the hotel living room area."

The regeneration program at Jaffa is a good example of the various ways communication with stakeholders can be undertaken. By demonstrating the benefits of properly caring for historic buildings Society for Protection of Israel Heritage Sites was able to engage persuade skeptical shop owners. Through education on the historical significance of the area by Eyal Ziv, the restoration architect, decision makers and the surrounding community were able to envision the advantages the regeneration program would provide. Although not the first regeneration project to be completed in the city -- one was completed during the 1960s and 1970s – the Jaffa program provides a successful continuation of the efforts of decades ago (Alfasi and Fabian 2009).

For the revelation awaits an appointed time; it speaks of the end and will not prove false. Though it linger, wait for it; it will certainly come and will not delay.
Habakkuk 2:3 NIV

In the end, the character of a civilization is encased in its structures.
--Frank Gehry, Architect

7 Conclusion

Stakeholders hold key positions in the revitalization process. Their involvement in planning is undoubtedly the greatest factor in a project's successful completion. The main focus of this text, stakeholders' roles have been described through the presentation of major revitalization projects in Durham, England, Bastrop, Louisiana (USA), and Jaffa, Israel. In the case of Durham, through the completion of a stakeholder analysis and the development of an influence map, more information was obtained to help resolve the challenges faced. The tools highlighted the need and value of early engagement of all levels of interest. This process of stakeholder research, however, could have additional parts. The stakeholder diagram illustrated previously, Figures 36 and 37, could potentially use a tertiary level in a project as complex as Durham, thus providing a concise way of viewing the wide range of stakeholders found. Subsequent tables, Tables 1 and 2, show that adding further details of the primary stakeholders would provide more value to the project. The additional levels of stakeholders and their information would provide more knowledge of what could be contributed to the program by a particular organization or group. Once the complete abilities and priorities are known, a list can be developed to demonstrate how each stakeholder can contribute to ensuring a successful outcome to the regeneration.

This approach leads back to the Burra Charter's emphasis on "the attachment of people to place, and the importance of their knowledge of the place" (Marquis-Kyle and Walker 2004). "Identifying the groups and individuals with special connections or interest in a place is part of the first step in the Burra Charter process," and in Durham this has been found to be influential in starting conversations among stakeholders and drawing them together. The consultations for the Market Place, for example, started a dialogue between the decision makers, Durham County Council and Durham City Vision, and the local community. It appeared that the consultations encouraged the same type of attention in other projects. At Elvet Waterside plans are set to develop more intense engagement with the community to establish what the needs are at the site. This will be essential in going forward.

Other revitalization projects such as the New Islington community in Manchester, England, also demonstrate that research into the wishes of stakeholders is important. The regeneration of the community included gathering the main ideas for the project from the residents (New Islington Client Group, nd). One of the greatest challenges was negating the views non-residents had of the area. Prior to redevelopment New Islington was a blighted area with dilapidated properties and an unsafe environment. The residents of the area struggled to resist the negative connotations.

Development company Urban Splash put renewed efforts into establishing a mixed-use area for diverse income levels, working directly with the residents to plan the revitalization project. Their "contributions were [noted as] key to the masterplan" (Urban Splash 2011). The managers of the project then created the overall design based on what the local community felt was vital. The final design featured two historic canals that flow through the location, period industrial structures, and a new residential building called "Chips" by prominent architect Will Alsop.

The revitalization of the city of Santa Cruz de Mompox (also known simply as Mompox) in the Momposino Depression in Colombia, South America, also demonstrates the significance of stakeholders. The historic colonial town lies along the Magdalena River and is surrounded by marshland making it accessible only by boat. Mompox has changed very little since early settlers and conquistadors established it in 1540, but the ancestral knowledge of the culture has been retained through its indigenous people (Gaviria Valenzuela 2013). Scholar Andres Gaviria Valenzuela and his team of researchers from Pontificia Universidad Javeriana are working in the town and outlying villages to research and develop a sustainable plan for development.

Gaviria Valenzuela has stated that outside the city centre the area lowlands suffer from increased incidents of flooding caused by global warming. In the highlands, however, drought conditions are common. A major challenge to renewing Mompox is developing a sensitive yet reliable means of transportation to the area. Mompox is so remote that emergency vehicles have difficulty accessing it. Moreover, many of the younger generation leave after graduating from high school, creating a large generation gap between those remaining.

Gaviria Valenzuela's research team is addressing these prevailing issues by encouraging Mompox citizens to take pride in preserving their heritage. The team has gained success in this by focusing on the area's unique vernacular architecture. It has obtained the intrinsic values of the stakeholders by asking such questions as What is significant to you? Valenzuela notes that design renderings of a thriving Mompox have been created based on information gained from residents. These renderings not only inspire residents and visitors but also stimulate dialogue on revitalization.

The idea of public value was an important topic in this publication as well. The city of Durham has numerous citizens who feel

Figure 76 New Islington (Manchester, England) prior to its regeneration (© *Urban Splash/Andrew Matthews*)

Figure 77 A larger multi-family housing building in New Islington, prior to its regeneration. (© *Urban Splash/Andrew Matthews*)

Figure 78 Apartment units in New Islington, after its regeneration. (© *Urban Splash*)

Figure 79 A newly contructed multi-family housing building in New Islington. (© *Urban Splash*)

strongly connected to the town, and their opinions carry tremendous influence. The exploration of this concept of public value within the Market Place site provided a window into the theory's complexities. It also illustrated the large role the decision maker has in the process. The act of educating the public to help its members make informed decisions on their heritage is a prime area for additional work. The act of educating the public to help its members make informed decisions on their heritage is valuable not only to the city involved but also to other urban areas beginning a revitalization project. Public value is a prime area for additional work.

One example of an educational initiative is to set up events where the value of the regeneration, specifically conservation, may be communicated and demonstrated "how it reflects the needs and values of the diverse publics it serves" (Blaug, Horner and Kekhi 2006). The use of these educational initiatives on an international scale would also promote their benefit to others working towards the same goals.

Durham's revitalization project has received mixed reviews thus far. The Durham Markets (located within the Marketplace) stated that foot traffic in the area has decreased by approximately ten percent, a decline that began during the construction phase of the project and continues. Although it has been noted that valuable new space has been created, the use of the area as an event location has thus far not been realized as fully as initially expected (Durham Markets 2013). Events such as a car show have taken place, but it is thought by businesses in the area that development of contemporary shopping markets outside the Marketplace have drawn residents and visitors outside the city center.

Further promotion of the role of conservation within the regeneration program will be important in developing aspects such as the buffer zone for the World Heritage site and a conservation area character appraisal to protect the historic assets in Durham. The

World Heritage site and the Georgian and Victorian layers of the city are part of Durham's identity. The aim of the regeneration program is to retain this character as well as create a modern environment in which people can live, work, and visit.

As noted at the beginning of this publication, many would like to see positive change in their geographic areas. The APA's report within the US noted that many would like to see improvement in safety, jobs, and city planning in their communities. Surveys have also been conducted in countries such as the UK that illustrate that heritage is highly valued. Individuals yearn for a place where they can feel safe, a place that exhibits character and has significance. A balance must be attained in planning. As real estate and economic development experts Donovan D. Rypkema and Caroline Cheong (2011) have stated, "Historic preservation is not about cities being the museums of yesterday; historic preservation is about using heritage resources to build quality of life for tomorrow." A safe and enjoyable life can be achieved by using the historic resources of a locale and engaging residents in the regeneration of the area.

The various levels of stakeholder engagement identified in Durham and in the international examples that followed illustrate the opportunities that are available. The incorporation of new approaches to the field such as those described and the continuation of successful methods that have been initiated will encourage success.

Whatever your hand finds to do, do it with all your might, for in the grave, where you are going, there is neither working nor planning nor knowledge nor wisdom.

Ecclesiastes 9:10 NIV

Bibliography

Published Sources

Abercrombie, P, Owens, J and Mealand, H A (1945) *A Plan for Bath*. London: Pitman.

Alfasi, N and Fabian, R (2009) 'Preserving Urban Heritage from Old Jaffa to Modern Tel-Aviv', *Israel Studies*, 14 (3), 137-156.

Araoz, G F (2008) 'World-Heritage Historic Urban Landscapes: Defining and Protecting Authenticity', *APT Bulletin*, 39 (2/3), 33-37.

BBC Wear (2 March 2010) 'County Durham's Haunted History', http://news.bbc.co.uk/local/wear/hi/people_and_places/history/newsid_8536000/8536853.stm. Page consulted 12 August 2010.

Blaug, R, Horner, L and Lekhi, R (2006) 'Heritage, Democracy and Public Value' in K Clark (ed), *Capturing the Public Value of Heritage: The Proceedings of the London Conference 25-26 January 2006*, 23-27. Swindon: English Heritage.

Bourne, L and Walker D H T (2005) 'Visualising and Mapping Stakeholder Influence', *Management Decision*, 43 (5), 649-660.

Boyle, J R (1892) *Comprehensive Guide to the County of Durham, with Maps and Plans*. London: Walter Scott Publishing.

Brandi, C (1963) 'Theory of Restoration, I-III' in N S Price, M K Talley Jr, and A M Vaccaro (eds), *Historical and Philosophical Issues in the Conservation of Cultural Heritage*, 230-235, 339-342, and 377-379. Los Angeles: J. Paul Getty Trust.

Central Bureau of Statistics (2009) *Statistical Abstract of Israel*. Jerusalem: Central Bureau of Statistics.

Chris Blandford Associates (2006) *Durham Cathedral and Castle World Heritage Site Management Plan*. Durham: One NorthEast.

City of Bastrop Louisiana (2007) 'City of Bastrop', http://www.cityofbastrop.com/. Page consulted 5 August 2010.

City of Durham Trust (2008) 'Elvet Waterside: Plans stalled', http://www.durhamcity.org/elvet_waterside.html. Page consulted 19 February 2010.

City of Durham Trust nd. 'Inspector's Report vindicates Trust', http://www.durhamcity.org/kascada.html. Page consulted 18 August 2010.

Clark, K (2001) *Informed Conservation: Understanding Historic Buildings and Their Landscapes for Conservation*. London: English Heritage.

Clark, K (ed) (2006a) *Capturing the Public Value of Heritage: The Proceedings of the London Conference 25-26 January 2006*. Swindon: English Heritage.

Clark, K (2006b) 'Introduction' in K Clark (ed), *Capturing the Public Value of Heritage: The Proceedings of the London Conference 25-26 January 2006*, 1-4. Swindon: English Heritage.

Clark, K and Maeer, G (2008) "The Cultural Value of Heritage: Evidence from the Heritage Lottery Fund, *Cultural Trends*, 17 (1), 23-56.

Clifford, C (6 September 2013) 'Life Advice from 18 of the Wealthiest People in History (Interactive Graphic)', *Entrepreneur Magazine* http://www.entrepreneur.com/article/228239#. Page consulted 27 October 2013.

Cramp, R and Scott, T (1987) 'Archaeology, Planning and Conservation in Durham: A United Kingdom Case Study' in Council of Europe (ed), *Archaeology and Planning: Report of the Florence Colloquy*, 39-53. Strasbourg: Council of Europe.

Cullingworth, J B and Nadin, V (2006) *Town and Country Planning in the UK*. Oxon: Routledge.

Delafons, J (1997) *Politics and Preservation: A Policy History of the Built Heritage, 1882-1996*. London: E. & F. N. Spon.

Department for Communities and Local Government (2010) *Planning for the Historic Environment*. London: The Stationery Office.

Department of the Environment (1990) *Archaeology and Planning*. London: HMSO.

Department of the Environment and Department of National Heritage (1994) *Planning and the Historic Environment*. London: HMSO.

Durham City Council nd. 'City of Durham Local Plan', http://www.cartoplus.co.uk/durham/text/00cont.htm. Page consulted 17 August 2010.

Durham City Vision (2007) *2020 Vision Durham City Centre: Durham City Centre Masterplan*. Durham: The Board of 2020 Vision Partnership.

Durham County Council (2004) *Conservation Areas*. Durham: Durham County Council.

Durham County Council (2010a) 'County Durham Plan - the Local Development Framework', http://www.durham.gov.uk/Pages/Service.aspx?ServiceId=856. Page consulted 1 August 2010.

Durham County Council (2010b) 'Durham Baths; site (Durham City)',
http://www.keystothepast.info/durhamcc/K2P.nsf/K2PDetail?readform&PRN=D15802. Page consulted 18 August 2010.

Durham County Council (2010c) 'Local Plans',
http://www.durham.gov.uk/Pages/Service.aspx?ServiceId=494. Page consulted 17 August 2010.

Durham County Council (2010d) 'Sustainable Design Supplementary Planning Document',
http://www.durham.gov.uk/pages/Service.aspx?ServiceId=7171. Page consulted 30 July 2010.

Durham Times (22 January 2010) 'Statue Move to Go Ahead After Consent Granted',
http://www.durhamtimes.co.uk/news/4866475.Statue_move_to_go_ahead_after_consent_granted/. Page consulted 13 July 2010.

Durham Times (14 May 2010) 'Renovation Begins As City Remains Open for Business',
http://www.durhamtimes.co.uk/news/8166341.Renovation_begins_as_city_remains_open_for_business/.
Page consulted 5 August 2010.

Durham University News (4 September 2008) 'Durham's World Heritage Site Expands',
http://www.dur.ac.uk/news/newsitem/?itemno=6941. Page consulted 5 August 2010.

Durham World Heritage Site (2014) 'Palace Green Library',
http://www.durhamworldheritagesite.com/architecture/palace-green/library. Page consulted 16 February 2014.

Encyclopædia Britannica Online (2010) 'Tel Aviv–Yafo', http://www.britannica.com/EBchecked/topic/585777/Tel-Aviv-Yafo. Page consulted 8 August 2010.

English Heritage (1998) *Conservation-led Regeneration: The Work of English Heritage*. London: English Heritage.

English Heritage (2005) *Regeneration and the Historic Environment: Heritage as a Catalyst for Better Social and Economic Regeneration*. London: English Heritage.

English Heritage (2006a) *Guidance on Conservation Area Appraisals*. Swindon: English Heritage.

English Heritage (2006b) *Guidance on the Management of Conservation Areas*. Swindon: English Heritage.

English Heritage (2008) *Conservation Principles: Policies and Guidance for the Sustainable Management of the Historic Environment*. London: English Heritage.

English Heritage (2009) *A Charter for English Heritage Planning and Development Advisory Services*. London: English Heritage.

Feilden, B M and Jokilehto, J (1998) *Management Guidelines for World Cultural Heritage Sites*. Rome: International Centre for the Study of the Preservation and Restoration of Cultural Property.

Giddens, A (1991) *Modernity and Self-Identity: Self and Society in the Late Modern Age*. Oxford: Polity Press.

Government Office for the Northeast (2002) *Regional Planning Guidance for the North East*. London: The Stationery Office.

Grenville, J (2007) 'Conservation as Psychology: Ontological Security and the Built Environment', *International Journal of Heritage Studies*, 13 (6), 447-461.

Helbling, W (5 June 2010) 'City to Sue Dixie Cleaners, Sell Hay', *Bastrop Enterprise,* http://www.bastropenterprise.com/news/x1143353877/City-to-sue-Dixie-Cleaners-sell-hay. Page consulted 8 August 2010.

Heritage Link (2004) *The Heritage Dynamo: How the voluntary sector drives regeneration.* London: Heritage Link.

Heritage Lottery Fund (2010) *Townscape Heritage Initiative: Grants of between £500,000 and £2 million, Introduction.* London: The Heritage Lottery Fund.

Hobson, E (2004) *Conservation and Planning: Changing Values in Policy and Practice.* London: Spon Press.

House of Commons (2004) *The Role of Historic Buildings in Urban Regeneration.* London: The Stationery Office.

Jagger, M (1998) 'The Planner's Perspective: A View from the Front' in J Warren, J Worthington, and S Taylor (eds), *Context: New Buildings in Historic Settings,* 71-82. Oxford: Architectural Press.

Jokilehto, J (1998) 'Organizations, Charters and World Movements -- An Overview' in J Warren, J Worthington, and S Taylor (eds), *Context: New Buildings in Historic Settings,* 40-50. Oxford: Architectural Press.

Jokilehto, J (1999) *A History of Architectural Conservation.* Oxford: Butterworth-Heinemann.

Jones, P and Evans, J (2008) *Urban Regeneration in the UK.* London: Sage.

Jowell, T (2006) 'From Consultation to Conversation: The Challenge of *Better Places to Live'* in K Clark (ed), *Capturing the Public Value of*

Heritage: The Proceedings of the London Conference 25-26 January 2006, 7-13. Swindon: English Heritage.

Kerr, J S (1990) *The Conservation Plan: A Guide to the Preparation of Conservation Plans for Places of European Cultural Significance.* Sydney: The National Trust of Australia.

Kersel, M M (2009) 'Walking a Fine Line: Obtaining Sensitive Information Using a Valid Methodology' in M L Stig Sørensen and J Carman (eds), *Heritage Studies: Methods and Approaches,* 178-200. Oxon: Routledge.

Larkham, P J (1996) *Conservation and the City.* London: Routledge.

Larkham, P J (2003) 'The Place of Urban Conservation in the UK Reconstruction Plans of 1942-1952', *Planning Perspectives,* 18 (3), 295-324.

Larkham P J and Lilley, K D (2003) 'Plans, Planners and City Images: Place Promotion and Civic Boosterism in British Reconstruction Planning', *Urban History,* 30 (2), 183-205.

LeBor, A (8 May 2008) 'Jaffa: Israel's Mixed City', *BBC News,* http://news.bbc.co.uk/1/hi/world/middle_east/7389512.stm. Page consulted 23 August 2010.

Lloyd, C (16 October 2009)'Hero or Villain?', *Durham Times,* http://www.durhamtimes.co.uk/leisure/features/4687689.Hero_or_villain_/. Page consulted 18 February 2010.

Madgin, R (2010) 'Reconceptualising the Historic Urban Environment: Conservation and Regeneration in Castlefield, Manchester, 1960-2009', *Planning Perspectives,* 25 (1), 29-48.

Marquis-Kyle, P and Walker, M (2004) *The Illustrated Burra Charter: Good Practice for Heritage Places.* Sydney: Australia ICOMOS.

Mayers, J and Vermeulen, S (2005) *Stakeholder Influence Mapping*. London: International Institute for Environment and Development.

Mayers, J (2005) *Stakeholder Power Analysis*. London: International Institute for Environment and Development.

Merriam-Webster Online Dictionary (2010) 'Communication', http://www.merriam-webster.com/dictionary/communication. Page consulted 14 July 2010.

Mind Tools (2010) 'Influence Maps', http://www.mindtools.com/pages/article/newPPM_83.htm. Page consulted 12 July 2010.

Moore, M H (1995) *Creating Public Value: Strategic Management in Government*. Cambridge: Harvard University Press.

Muñoz Viñas, S (2005) *Contemporary Theory of Conservation*. Oxford: Elsevier.

Mynors, C (2006) *Listed buildings, Conservation Areas and Monuments*. London: Sweet and Maxwell.

National Conference of State Historic Preservation Officers nd. 'Best Practices: Quotations on the importance of history and historic preservation', http://www.ncshpo.org/current/quotes.htm. Page consulted 27 October 2013.

National Park Service nd. 'Using the Standards and Guidelines', http://www.nps.gov/hps/tps/standguide/overview/using_standguide.htm. Page consulted 5 August 2010.

National Trust for Historic Preservation (2009) 'The Main Street Four-Point Approach', http://www.preservationnation.org/main-street/about-main-street/the-approach/. Page consulted 8 August 2010.

New Islington Client Group nd. 'Regeneration of A Community', http://www.newislington.co.uk/whats-it-all-about/regeneration-of-a-community/. Page consulted 10 August 2010.

Office for National Statistics (2004) *Census 2001: Key Statistics for Urban Areas in the North*. London: The Stationery Office.

Office for National Statistics (2005) 'Glossary of Terms', http://www.statistics.gov.uk/census2001/glossary.asp#ua. Page consulted 5 August 2010.

Orbaşli, A (2008) *Architectural Conservation*. Oxford: Blackwell Publishing.

Otero-Pailos, J, Gaiger, J and West, S (2010) 'Heritage Values' in S West (ed), *Understanding Heritage In Practice*, 47-87. Manchester: Manchester University Press.

Pendlebury, J (2003) 'Planning the Historic City: Reconstruction Plans in the United Kingdom in the 1940s', *The Town Planning Review*, 74 (4), 371-393.

Pendlebury, J (2009) *Conservation and the Age of Consensus*. Oxon: Routledge.

Petts, D, Gerrard, C and Cranstone, D (2006) *Shared Visions: The North-East Regional Research Framework for the Historic Environment*. Durham: Durham County Council.

Pevsner, N (1983) *County Durham*. London: Penguin.

Pocock, D (1999) *Durham: Essays on Sense of Place*. Durham: City of Durham Trust.

Pocock, D (2006) *The Futures of Durham: A Reflective Essay*. Durham: City of Durham Trust.

Povoledo, E (2 June 2012) 'Quakes Deal Irreparable Blow to an Italian Region's Cultural Heritage', *The New York Times*, http://www.nytimes.com/2012/06/03/world/europe/italy-assesses-damage-to-cultural-heritage.html Page Consulted 10 June 2012.

Power of Place Office (2000) *Power of Place: The Future of the Historic Environment*. London: Power of Place Office.

Resig, D (2012) 'Nehemiah -- The Man Behind the Wall', http://www.biblicalarchaeology.org/daily/people-cultures-in-the-bible/people-in-the-bible/nehemiah%E2%80%93the-man-behind-the-wall/. Page consulted 22 November 2013.

Richardson, A (22 August 2013) 'Regeneration of former ice rink starts', *The Northern Echo*, http://www.thenorthernecho.co.uk/business/news/10628958.print/. Page consulted 26 November 2013.

Riegl, A (1903) 'The Modern Cult of Monuments: Its Essence and Its Development' in N S Price, M K Talley Jr, and A M Vaccaro (eds), *Historical and Philosophical Issues in the Conservation of Cultural Heritage*, 69-83. Los Angeles: J. Paul Getty Trust.

Roberts, P (2000) 'The Evolution, Definition and Purpose of Urban Regeneration' in P Roberts and H Sykes (eds), *Urban Regeneration: A handbook*, 9-36. London: Sage.

Royal Institution of Chartered Surveyors (2008) *Heritage Works: The Use of Historic Buildings in Regeneration; A Toolkit of Good Practice.* London: English Heritage.

Ruskin, J (1849) 'The Lamp of Memory, I' in N S Price, M K Talley Jr, and A M Vaccaro (eds), *Historical and Philosophical Issues in the Conservation of Cultural Heritage*, 42-43. Los Angeles: J. Paul Getty Trust.

Rypkema, D and Cheong, C (2011) *Measuring the Economics of Preservation: Recent Findings.* Washington, DC: Advisory Council on Historic Preservation.

Sharp, T (1940) *Town Planning.* Harmondsworth: Penguin Books.

Sharp, T (1945) *Cathedral City: A Plan for Durham.* London: Architectural Press.

Shipley, R, Reeve, A, Walker, S, Grover, P and Goodey, B (2004) 'Townscape Heritage Initiatives Evaluation: Methodology for Assessing the Effectiveness of Heritage Lottery Fund Projects in the United Kingdom', *Environment and Planning C: Government and Policy*, 22, 523-542.

Society for the Protection of Ancient Buildings (2009) 'The Manifesto', http://www.spab.org.uk/what-is-spab-/the-manifesto/. Page consulted 15 August 2010.

Stig Sørensen, M L and Carman, J (2009) 'Introduction: Making the Means Transparent: Reasons and Reflections' in M L Stig Sørensen and J Carman (eds), *Heritage Studies: Methods and Approaches*, 3-10. Oxon: Routledge.

Tait, M and Campbell, H (2000) 'The Politics of Communication Between Planning Officers and Politicians: The Exercise of Power Through Discourse', *Environment and Planning A*, 32, 489-506.

Tallentire, M (9 April 2010) 'Blind Say Market Place Plan is Accident Waiting to Happen', *The Northern Echo*, http://www.thenorthernecho.co.uk/news/local/durham/8089892Blind_say_market_place_plan_is_accident_waiting_to_happen/undefined/. Page consulted 5 August 2010.

Tallentire, M (10 June 2010) 'Concern Over City Baths', *The Northern Echo*, http://www.thenorthernecho.co.uk/news/local/durham/8213535.Concern_over_city_baths/. Page consulted 13 July 2010.

Tallentire, M (30 March 2012) 'City regeneration group is scrapped', *The Northern Echo*, http://www.thenorthernecho.co.uk/news/9622129.print/. Page consulted 19 November 2013.

Tallentire, M (11 September 2013) 'City masterplan aims to attract £850m investment', *The Northern Echo*, http://www.thenorthernecho.co.uk/news/local/northdurham/10668613.City_masterplan_aims_to_attract__850m_investment/?ref=rss. Page consulted 20 November 2013.

Tallentire, M (7 October 2013) 'Have your say on Durham masterplan', *The Northern Echo*, http://www.thenorthernecho.co.uk/news/10722709.Have_your_say_on_Durham_masterplan/?ref=rc. Page consulted 19 November 2013.

UNESCO (2013) 'New Life For Historic Cities: The Historic Urban Landscape Approach Explained' http://whc.unesco.org/en/activities/727. Page consulted 12 February 2014.

UNESCO World Heritage Centre (2010) 'International Expert meeting on World Heritage and buffer zones' http://whc.unesco.org/en/events/473/. Page consulted 18 August 2010.

UNESCO World Heritage Centre (2012) 'New Recommendation on the Historic Urban Landscape' http://whc.unesco.org/en/news/873/. Page consulted 12 February 2014.

Urban Task Force (1999) *Towards an Urban Renaissance*. London: Spon.

Urban Task Force (2005) 'Towards a Strong Urban Renaissance', http://www.urbantaskforce.org/UTF_final_report.pdf. Page consulted 20 July 2010.

Urban Splash (2011) 'New Islington', http://www.urbansplash.co.uk/residential/new-islington. Page consulted 5 January 2014.

Viollet-le-duc, E (1854) 'Restoration' in N S Price, M K Talley Jr, and A M Vaccaro (eds), *Historical and Philosophical Issues in the Conservation of Cultural Heritage*, 314-318. Los Angeles: J. Paul Getty Trust.

West, S and Ansell, J (2010) 'A History of Heritage' in S West (ed), *Understanding Heritage In Practice*, 7-46. Manchester: Manchester University Press.

Your Shout Communications (2009) *Heart of the City: Durham Market Place and Vennels Consultation Summary Report March 2009*. Durham: Durham City Vision.

Archival Sources & Interviews

Adkins, L (2010) National Main Street Program. [Interview]. March 2010.

Alford-Olive, B (2010) Bastrop Revitalization Project. [Interview]. May 2010.

Arnett, S (2010) Bastrop Revitalization Project. [Interview]. May 2010

Downs, C (2010) Durham Cathedral & Durham Regeneration Program. [Interview]. June 2010.

Duckworth, N (2010) Conservation & the Durham Regeneration Program. [Interview]. May 2010.

Durham County Council, Elvet Waterside Planning and Conservation Area Consent Files, 08/00003/FPA, 2010.

Durham County Council, Ice Rink Planning and Conservation Area Consent Files, 05/00207/FPA, 2006.

Durham County Council, Market Place Planning and Listed Building Consent Files, 09/00535/FPA, 2009.

Durham County Record Office, Durham City Council, HTP 4/54, Elvet Waterside Re-development, 1/211/4/1,1961-1962.

Durham County Record Office, Durham County Council (1888 - 1974), CC/Planning 1297, Durham M.B., Development North and South Claypath, 31 January 1969 - 11 June 1969.

Durham County Record Office, Durham County Council (1888 - 1974), CC/Planning 1298, Durham M.B., Conservation Area, Article 4 Direction --Correspondence with County Clerk and City of Durham Trust, 11 July 1969 - 20 November 1969.

Durham County Record Office, Durham District Council, ND/Du 13/6, 13/109 and 13/208, Plans submitted to local authority, 17 November 1901, 23 December 1909 and 13 September 1920.

El-Rashidi, S (2010) Durham World Heritage Site. [Interview]. June 2010.

El-Rashidi, S (2013) Durham World Heritage Site & Regeneration Program. [Interview]. August 2013.

English Heritage, Former Ice Rink site file, CHA/5197/0004, 2006.

Farmer, W P (2013) *Adding, Preserving and Subtracting: The Art of City-building.* [Conference lecture]. US/ICOMOS. Savannah, Georgia USA, 1-4 May 2013.

Gaviria Valenzuela, A (2013) Revitalization of the city of Santa Cruz de Mompox. [Interview]. May 2013.

Hammerton, B (2010) *An introduction to project management, with case studies (The Cutty Sark).* [Lecture]. 17 February 2010, Conservation Solutions module, University of York.

Hedley, C (2010) Durham Regeneration Program & Handicap Accessibility. [Interview]. June 2010.

Herbert, P (2010) Durham Regeneration & Planning. [Interview]. May 2010.

Hilland, P (1978) 'Values and architectural conservation', unpublished Diploma dissertation, University of York.

Hunter, A (2010) Durham Regeneration Program. [Interview]. June 2010.

Hurlow, M (2010) Design & the Durham Regeneration Program. [Interview]. May 2010 & July 2010.

Inch, A (2010) The Durham Regeneration Program. [Interview]. June 2010.

King, K (2010) Bastrop Economic Development Program. [Interview]. May 2010

Ritson, K L (2009) 'Preservation planning at the local level: a case study analysis', unpublished MS thesis, University of Pennsylvania.

Robinson, P (2010) Durham Regeneration. [Interview]. June 2010.

Tuchler, T (2010) Jaffa Revitalization Project. [Interview]. March 2010.

Vereen, M Bastrop Main Street Program. [Interview]. May 2010.

Wilkes, C (2010) Durham Regeneration Program and the Business Community. [Interview]. June 2010.

Zevi, R (2010) Jaffa Revitalization Project. [Interview]. March 2010.

Video Sources

BBC News (2008) In video: Jaffa Stories, The Architect, internet video, 8 May 2008, http://news.bbc.co.uk/1/hi/world/middle_east/7388445.stm#architect. Page consulted 9 August 2010.

Appendices

A. Completing A Stakeholder Analysis

This section will provide details on how the stakeholder analysis was completed for the Durham case study. It will serve as an example of how the method may be incorporated into other revitalization projects of historic places. The preliminary step was to understand the context of the revitalization. This was valuable in gaining an overall view of the project's elements, the role of conservation within it, and the challenges that developed.

The preliminary step in the analysis requires the identification of key stakeholders (Mayers 2005). There are general stakeholder groups in most projects of this type: the media, residents, and temporary residents (i.e. students, tourists, etc.), and a historic preservation or civic non-governmental/non-profit group. The stakeholders in the Durham analysis were chosen primarily by looking at the previous types of organizations, including those managing the regeneration--Durham City Vision and Durham County Council--and reviewing the most vocal groups regarding the development of the three sites. All had participated in varying levels with the areas investigated.

Following the identification of the stakeholders, additional techniques were implemented as part of the stakeholder analysis portion of the research. Included in the approach was the completion of semi-structured interviews with the stakeholders involved. Questions presented were constructed to gain general information about interviewees' roles in conservation and planning within their respective organizations. They were aimed to obtain particulars on each of the cases that were part of the revitalization project and to ascertain their views on the development of each site--the challenges that arose, the solutions that were foreseen, and the current state of planning for the sites.

> Sample Questions from Semi-Structured Interviews:
> • What is the mission of your department/organization?
>
> • How were comments or questions from your department/organization delivered to other stakeholders?
>
> • What are the challenges you foresee for the regeneration program?

The analysis was a tool used to understand and gain detailed information on the stakeholders and their relationships with each other, thus revealing the causes of challenges reported within the program. Controversial projects require focusing attention on understanding a problem at the surface level and then examining the specifics that underlie possible problems that have occurred. After these issues were determined, a starting point was created from which to build solutions to the problems faced by those involved. This process allowed an analysis of what the stakeholders valued, their position in the project, and the outcomes that they foresaw for the particular sites in which they were involved. It also helped to ascertain their views of the regeneration program in general.

The individuals and organizations located were also found through a review of newspaper articles on the program and an examination of the recent census to learn about those making up the residential stakeholder group within the city. Valuable background knowledge was obtained from reviewing these documents.

The production of a diagram, depicted in Figures 36 and 37, was necessary after the identification of the stakeholders to highlight those who were potentially affected by the circumstances and interested in the outcomes of the cases ("secondary stakeholders") and those whose participation would be vital to the development and completion of the project ("primary stakeholders") (Mayers 2005). The location of the stakeholders in the diagram was confirmed after completion of the influence map discussed in the following section.

An important aspect of the analysis required an investigation of the makeup of the stakeholder groups within the local community. The 2001 UK Census records were surveyed to determine the demographics of Durham. This data provided a perspective of who resided in the town and would have an interest in the regeneration. Another aspect of the research was an evaluation of the literature developed for the present regeneration program and for previous conservation and planning initiatives within the city. The city's master plan for the regeneration was reviewed along with the archives of the Durham County Record Office, several dissertations completed on Durham at the University of York, and the holdings of the Durham University Library. The documents provided an overall image of the current and past roles of conservation and planning in the history of Durham. This step also contributed to the stakeholder analysis as the previous work provided an opportunity to investigate the opinions of the immediate community and the character of the city prior to the present program.

B. The Influence Map

As various levels of the local community were involved in the program -- the public sector, the non-profit sector, private businesses, and individuals -- it was important to assess the influence each had on the outcome of the regeneration. The review of the cases and semi-structured interviews illustrated where the influences existed. The evaluation revealed which stakeholders were exerting influence in relation to others throughout the project. This knowledge helped to distinguish where future emphasis needed to be placed to promote favorable results. An influence map, a tool created to depict the influences within a project, was completed to achieve this outcome, Figures 34 and 35 (Mayers and Vermeulen 2005).

The influence map provided a diagram in which each stakeholder was depicted with arcs radiating from each, providing a visual representation of the direction of their influence. The width of the arcs illustrated the nature of the influence, with the wider arcs depicting greater influence. The color signified the type; for example, amber encouraged caution, red represented a possible stop in the process, and green represented fluidity of actions and communication among an organization or group with other stakeholders.

About the Author

Lydia Atubeh received her master's degree from the University of York (York, England) in Conservation Studies (Historic Buildings). Atubeh is a member of the DeKalb County Historic Preservation Commission (Decatur, GA), a member of the United States International Council on Monuments and Sites (US/ICOMOS), and has taught International Heritage Preservation at Georgia State University (Atlanta, GA).

Connect with Lydia Atubeh

Twitter: @Lydia_K_A

LinkedIn: www.**linkedin**.com/in/**lydiaatubeh**

Website: www.kenlchaimhistoricbuildings.com

www.ingramcontent.com/pod-product-compliance
Lightning Source LLC
Chambersburg PA
CBHW042056290426
44111CB00001B/20